BACK ROADS
OF OREGON

Happy Birthday
July 2, 1986
Aunt Peg

Dog barn at Cornucopia

# Back Roads of Oregon

by Earl Thollander

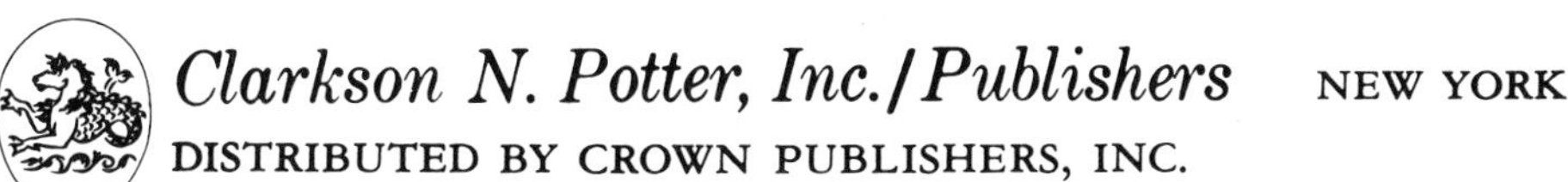

Clarkson N. Potter, Inc./Publishers NEW YORK
DISTRIBUTED BY CROWN PUBLISHERS, INC.

Books by Earl Thollander

BACK ROADS OF NEW ENGLAND
BACK ROADS OF OREGON
BACK ROADS OF ARIZONA
BACK ROADS OF CALIFORNIA
BARNS OF CALIFORNIA
BACK ROADS OF TEXAS

FRONT COVER: Ranch near Galena on the middle fork of the John Day



Inquiries should be addressed to Clarkson N. Potter, Inc., One Park Avenue, New York, N.Y. 10016
Printed in the United States of America
Published simultaneously in Canada by
General Publishing Company Limited

Library of Congress Cataloging in Publication Data
Thollander, Earl.
Back roads of Oregon.
1. Oregon—Description and travel—1951–
—Guide-books. 2. Automobiles—Road guides—Oregon.
I. Title.
F874.3.T48 1979 917.95'04'4 78-24097
ISBN: 0-517-530694 (cloth)
0-517-537818 (paper)
10 9 8 7 6 5 4 3 2

*I dedicate this book,
with much love, to my
family--Janet, Kristie,
Wes and Lauren*

# Contents



## Back Roads of Southwestern Oregon

Back Roads of Northwestern Oregon

*Back Roads of Eastern Oregon*



*Map legend*

3.2 distance in miles between dots
→ → → my route (which may be reversed should you desire)
▲ campgrounds
■ towns and cities
............... rivers and lake boundaries
□ special location
× my sketching place
covered bridge
π picnic grounds
cemetery

NORTH is always toward the top of the page

## FOREWORD

Oregon is a state with many faces. It is a state of matchless beauty and bountiful resources.

Oregonians are proud of their state. A commonsense approach to problem solving, balanced budgets, and unique environmental laws are all part of the Oregon experience.

Oregon is unique. Mountains, trees, and rocky coves to the west, with deserts and sage to the east. Much of this state's beauty and charm can only be found by the interested explorer who probes beyond the obvious.

Earl Thollander has made a substantial investment of his time and artistic talent in this state. His illustrations and text will convince even the casual reader that there is a valuable reward waiting for those willing to venture off the well-traveled path to search quietly and patiently through Oregon's many special places.

Read and enjoy this guide to the back roads of this state. As governor of Oregon I invite you to experience for yourself the joys of discovery felt by the author as he traveled our country roads. If you have never been to Oregon, I know you will fall in love with our state. If you are a native, a whole new state awaits discovery along the back roads of Oregon.

February, 1979 — Governor Vic Atiyeh

# Preface

*Back Roads of Oregon* is a travel guide, an on-the-spot pictorial record of landscapes and places seen, and an effort to give "voice" to the back road beauty of Oregon. For me there is more of nature, more experience of the earth, a greater feeling of history, and more good adventures to be had by getting off the main thoroughfares and away from urban centers.

I drew this book not only because of an urge to describe to everyone what wonderful things I have seen in Oregon, but also to help others, in my small way, discover the beauty of the natural world. Without strong support from concerned people, preserving and managing the natural areas that remain will be difficult. Indeed without care and help we will someday create a less interesting and less habitable planet.

# Author's Note

The three parts of Back Roads of Oregon begin with a sectional map. This will help to locate the back roads areas on a larger Oregon state map that is available at no charge from many sources, including Travel Services, Chambers of Commerce, Tourist Bureaus and Automobile Clubs. My more localized maps in each section outline every back road and should successfully guide you in your trip. I have put as much information as I could manage into the maps themselves. Arrows show you the direction in which I traveled, although my route could certainly be reversed. The North Pole, unless otherwise indicated, is toward the top of the page. Maps are not to scale because of the diversity in length of the roads; however, mileage notations should help a great deal. My odometer wouldn't have measured distance exactly the same as yours, but their estimates should be similar. Essential to me in following the back roads were sectional maps, which I purchased from the Oregon Department of Transportation, Room 17, Transportation Building, Salem, Oregon 97310. Pasted together, the various sections of a county map, at one-half inch to the mile, would achieve monumental proportions. Malheur County alone, for example, measured 30 x 75 inches!

I also purchased maps at ranger stations when entering forest preserves. They are a bit more complete than the Department's sectional maps in that forest road numbers are included.

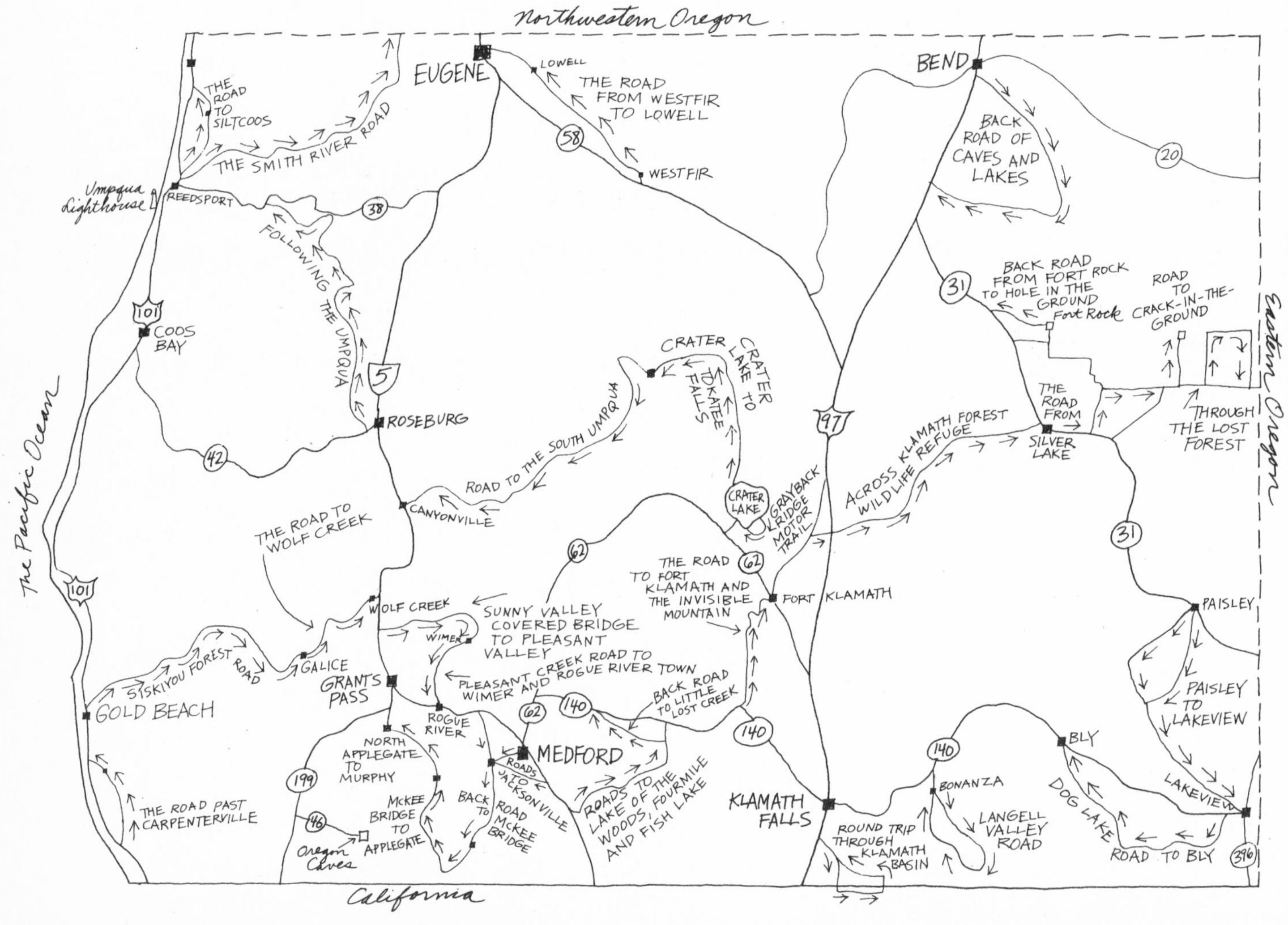

Northwestern Oregon
Eastern Oregon
California
The Pacific Ocean
EUGENE
LOWELL
THE ROAD FROM WESTFIR TO LOWELL
58
WESTFIR
BEND
BACK ROAD OF CAVES AND LAKES
20
THE ROAD TO SILTCOOS
THE SMITH RIVER ROAD
Umpqua Lighthouse
REEDSPORT
38
FOLLOWING THE UMPQUA
101
COOS BAY
5
ROSEBURG
42
CRATER
CRATER LAKE TO TOKATEE FALLS
ROAD TO THE SOUTH UMPQUA
CANYONVILLE
THE ROAD TO WOLF CREEK
97
31
BACK ROAD FROM FORT ROCK TO HOLE IN THE GROUND
Fort Rock
ROAD TO CRACK-IN-THE-GROUND
THE ROAD FROM SILVER LAKE
THROUGH THE LOST FOREST
ACROSS KLAMATH FOREST WILDLIFE REFUGE
CRATER LAKE
GRAYBACK RIDGE MOTOR TRAIL
62
THE ROAD TO FORT KLAMATH AND THE INVISIBLE MOUNTAIN
FORT KLAMATH
WOLF CREEK
SUNNY VALLEY COVERED BRIDGE TO PLEASANT VALLEY
WIMER
SISKIYOU FOREST ROAD
GALICE
GRANTS PASS
GOLD BEACH
PLEASANT CREEK ROAD TO WIMER AND ROGUE RIVER TOWN
ROGUE RIVER
BACK ROAD TO LITTLE LOST CREEK
140
MEDFORD
NORTH APPLEGATE TO MURPHY
ROADS TO JACKSONVILLE
McKEE BRIDGE TO APPLEGATE
BACK TO McKEE BRIDGE
ROAD
ROADS TO LAKE OF THE WOODS, FOURMILE AND FISH LAKE
199
46
Oregon Caves
THE ROAD PAST CARPENTERVILLE
KLAMATH FALLS
ROUND TRIP THROUGH KLAMATH BASIN
BONANZA
LANGELL VALLEY ROAD
BLY
DOG LAKE
ROAD TO BLY
PAISLEY
PAISLEY TO LAKEVIEW
LAKEVIEW
396

Rhododendron

# Southwestern Oregon

I remember the beauty and force of the ocean coast, the forests gleaming with dew in the morning light, the sumptuous displays of mountain wildflowers, and the textural infinity of sagebrush mixed with pines and junipers in the high, dry portion of southwestern Oregon.

OREGON
CHEDDAR
CHEESE
W. J. WALKER & SO

Cheese factory at Pistol River

# The road past Carpenterville

Old Highway 101, called the Carpenterville Road, wound above the ocean through lush, green coastal forest. It becomes a ridge route at times, with long views on both sides of the road, but don't expect a town at Carpenterville! Just north of Pistol River I drew a picture of a cheese factory of an earlier day being "consumed" by wild blackberry bushes.

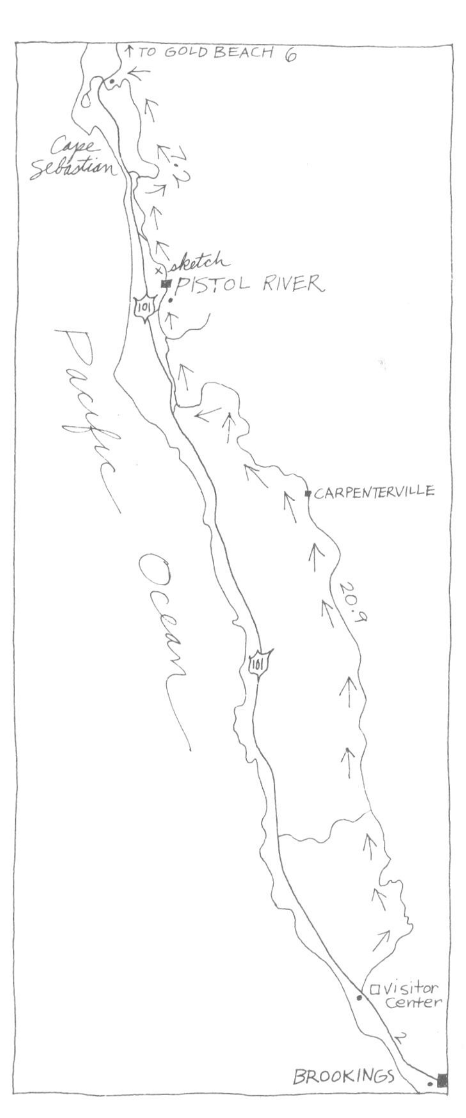
↑TO GOLD BEACH 6
Cape Sebastian
7.2
sketch
PISTOL RIVER
101
Pacific Ocean
CARPENTERVILLE
20.9
101
Visitor Center
2
BROOKINGS

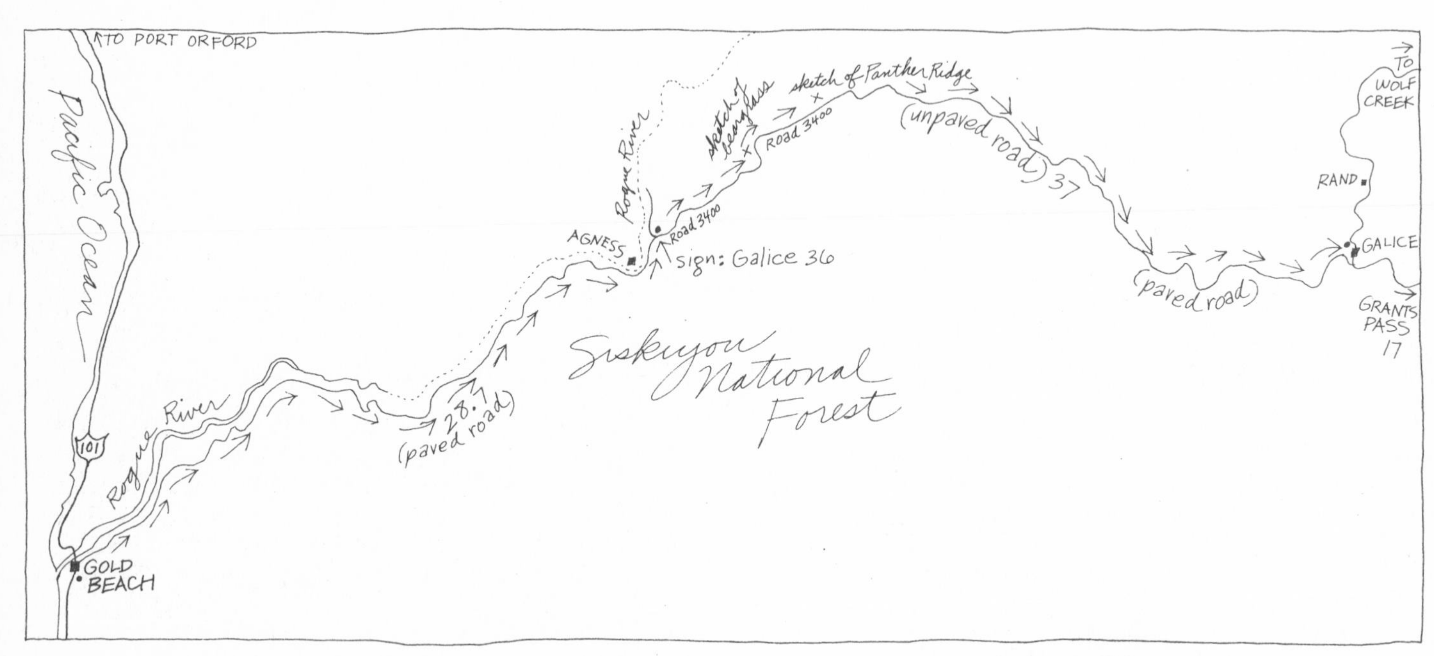
TO PORT ORFORD
Pacific Ocean
101
Rogue River
GOLD BEACH
28.7
(paved road)
Siskiyou National Forest
AGNESS
Rogue River
Road 3400
sign: Galice 36
sketch of beargrass
Road 3400
sketch of Panther Ridge
(unpaved road) 37
(paved road)
TO WOLF CREEK
RAND
GALICE
GRANTS PASS 17

Stonecrop

## Siskiyou Forest Road, Gold Beach to Galice

I stopped at Gold Beach Ranger Station for a Siskiyou National Forest map and to ask for advice on the current condition of the road beyond Agness.

The road along the Rogue River was paved for the first twenty-nine miles.

I saw a power boat moving upstream at almost the same speed as I was traveling.

Past Agness a gravel road wound its way through the forest. Eventually I came across an area of many beargrass plants in blossom. There, on the white flower I selected to draw, I discovered a perfectly camouflaged white spider that had captured an unsuspecting wasp.

I had expansive views of mountains and forest for my drawing of Panther Ridge.

Beargrass

Panther Ridge

WILLIAM
MILLER
TENNESSEE

*Headstone at Wolf Creek cemetery*

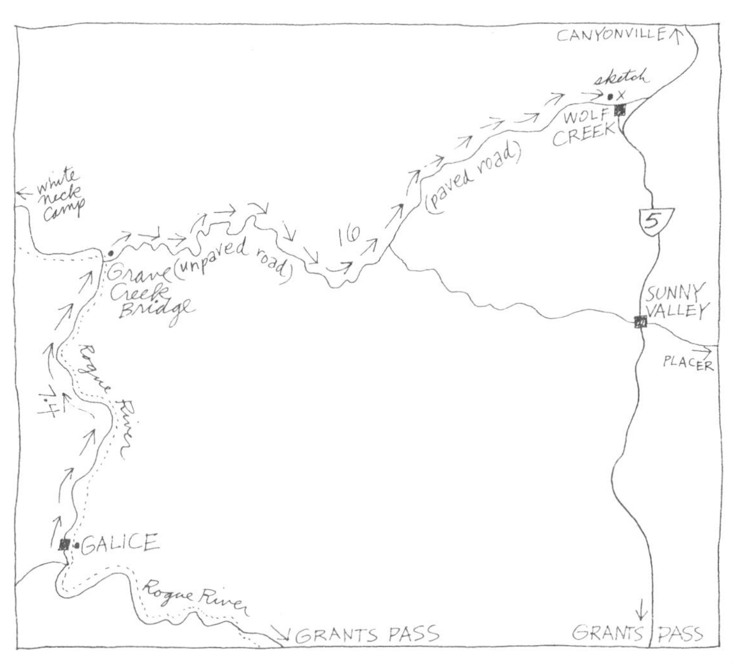

CANYONVILLE
sketch
WOLF CREEK
(paved road)
16
white neck Camp
Grave Creek Bridge
(unpaved road)
5
SUNNY VALLEY
PLACER
Rogue River
7.4
GALICE
Rogue River
GRANTS PASS
GRANTS PASS


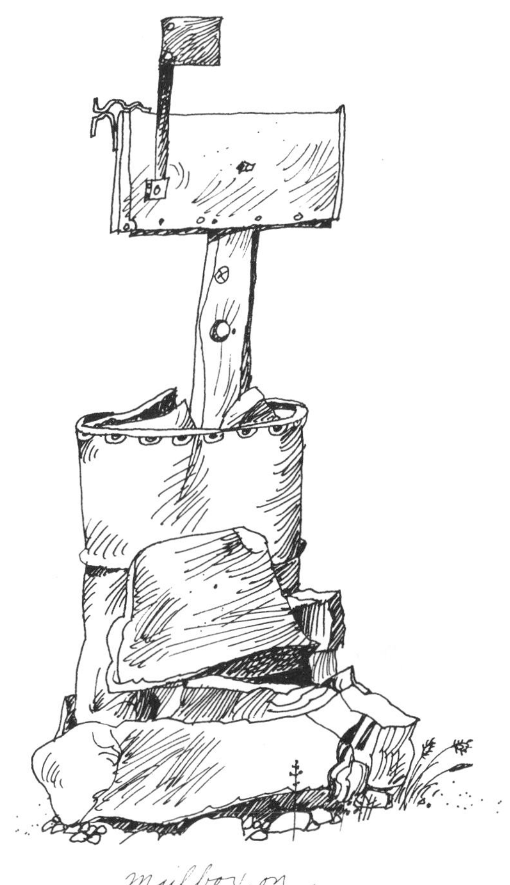

Mailbox on Wolf Creek road

# The road to Wolf Creek

I took the road north from Galice along the Rogue, turning east at Grave Creek Bridge. In five miles I passed a nicely made log barn and also a sign that said "No shooting children and livestock." Turning at the fork of the road toward Wolf Creek, I traveled along the pretty stream to the sleepy town ahead where old Wolf Creek Tavern (1857) still stands. On a hill nearby I sat in the deep shade of the town cemetery to sketch an ivy-covered headstone.

## Sunny Valley covered bridge to Pleasant Valley

Sunny Valley covered bridge crosses Grave Creek, so named in memory of a fourteen-year-old pioneer, buried nearby, a member of the first wagon train to enter Oregon by the Applegate Trail in 1846.

A small boy I met who lived on a farm along the road told me that there were beavers in the creek.

I got advice along the way from local folks and abandoned the Daisy Mine Road upon hearing their cautionary "This yere road's so rough ye could berry yer wheel in one 'o them holes."

Meadows along Ditch Creek Road were sprinkled with countless daisies blooming in late spring.

Sunny Valley covered bridge

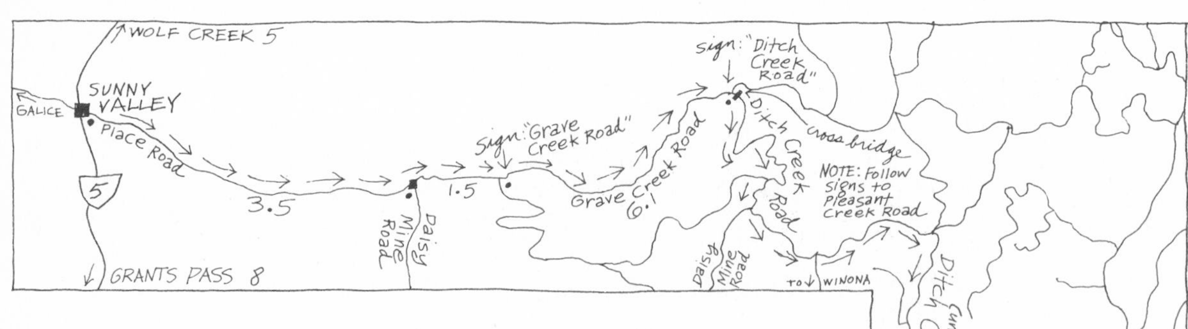
WOLF CREEK 5
SUNNY VALLEY
GALICE
Place Road
5
3.5
Daisy Mine Road
1.5
Sign: "Grave Creek Road"
Grave Creek Road
6.1
sign: "Ditch Creek Road"
Ditch Creek Road
cross bridge
NOTE: Follow signs to Pleasant Creek Road
Daisy Mine Road
TO WINONA
GRANTS PASS 8

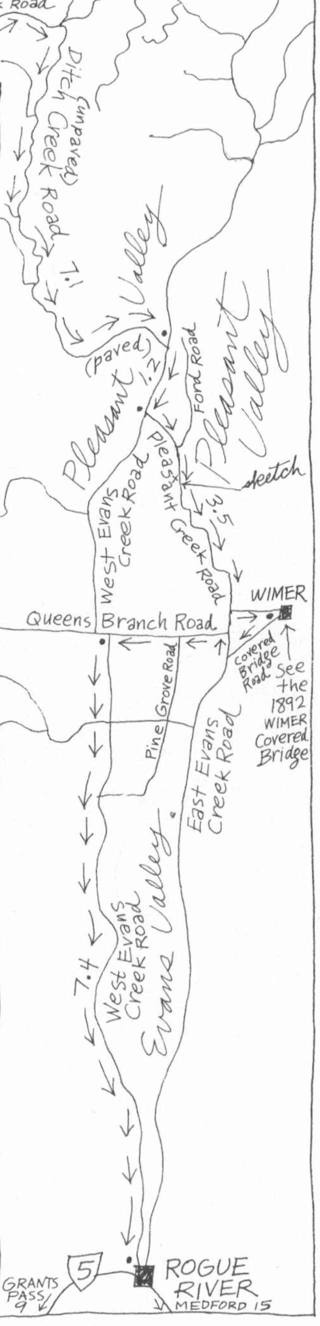
Ditch Creek Road (unpaved)
7.1
Valley
(paved)
Pleasant
1.2
Ford Road
Pleasant Valley
Pleasant Creek Road
3.5
sketch
West Evans Creek Road
Queens Branch Road
WIMER
Covered Bridge Road
See the 1892 WIMER Covered Bridge
Pine Grove Road
East Evans Creek Road
7.4
West Evans Creek Road
Evans Valley
GRANTS PASS 9
5
ROGUE RIVER
MEDFORD 15

## *Pleasant Creek Road to Wimer and Rogue River town*

At 2383 Pleasant Creek Road I sketched a portion of a collection of old structures and felt fully immersed in the spirit of Oregon's past. Grapevines and roses flourished, and peacocks, ducks, cats, and a friendly dog roamed about the thick grass.

farm on Pleasant Creek Road

# Roads to Jacksonville

Jacksonville is a ghost town revived by a remarkable number of handsome restored houses and other edifices that are worth seeing.

David Rust's place, recognizable by the colossal swans on its porch, is not on the usual tour of Jacksonville.

He said if I brought him the base of a hollow log and the crotch of a tree with the right curve in it, he'd make one for me.

380
RUST

Swan house, Jacksonville

GOLD HILL
5
99
12
62
5
5.5
RUCH 8
238
5
MEDFORD
238
JACKSONVILLE
99
TO
BUNCOM
8
ASHLAND
16

 St. Joseph's Church, Jacksonville

Roads to Jacksonville

St. Joseph's Church (1858) at 4th and D streets in Jacksonville was on the list of things to see. It's a historical place, as you can tell from this excerpt from a report by the town's first Catholic missionary to his superior, Archbishop Francis Blanchet ...

Sept. 18, 1856

... the Catholics in Jacksonville are very anxious to have a church built amongst them and are willing to help to the utmost of their means. I have given them some hopes of having their wishes realized next year... Next spring, if the mining be successful this winter, there would be a fair chance of making a good collection toward building a little church, which will answer not only for that town but for all the mining districts for 60 or 70 miles all around.

# Back road from Jacksonville to Buncom and McKee Bridge

This was a pleasant trip past stream and forest. At ghostly Buncom cows grazed in the green meadow where the town once stood. Next, I traveled along the Little Applegate River, and then by the big Applegate to McKee Bridge.

The covered bridge was built in 1917 when the Blue Ledge Copper Mine was still transporting ore to Jacksonville.

I could hear the swishing sound of a rotary fish screen operating much like an old-fashioned water wheel as I sketched. The screen prevents trout from going out of the river into irrigation canals and ending up "dried out" in a pasture somewhere.

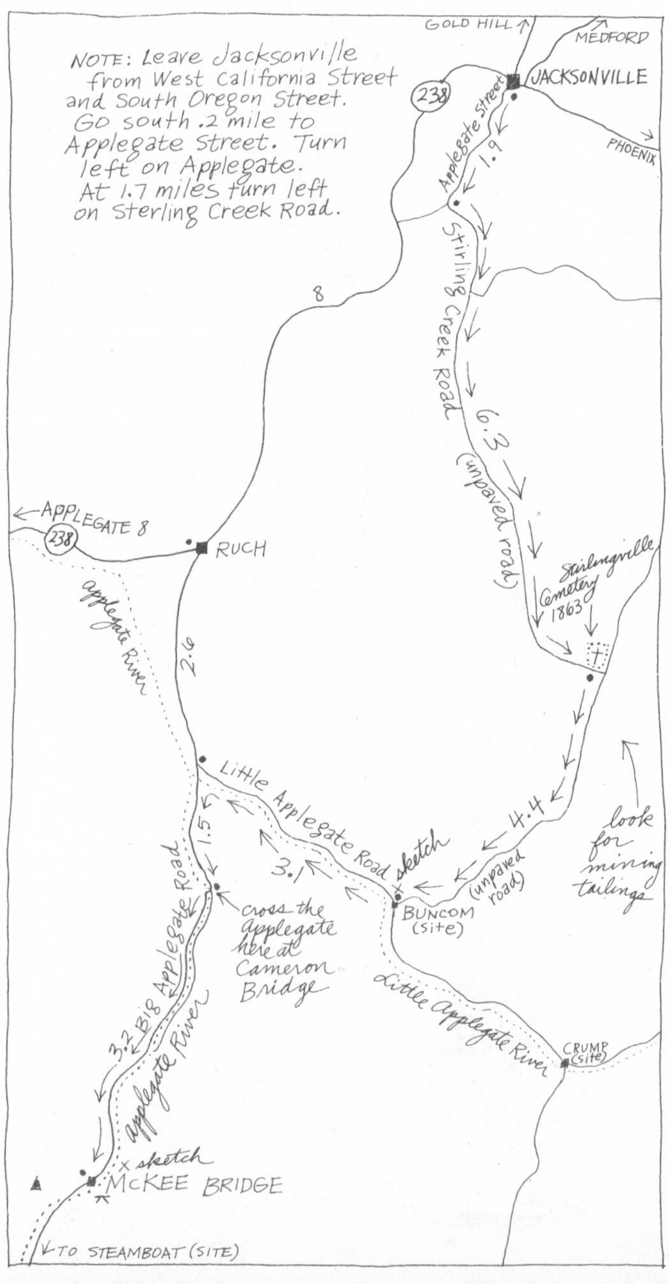
NOTE: Leave Jacksonville from West California Street and South Oregon Street. Go south .2 mile to Applegate Street. Turn left on Applegate. At 1.7 miles turn left on Sterling Creek Road.
GOLD HILL
MEDFORD
JACKSONVILLE
PHOENIX
238
Applegate Street
1.9
Stirling Creek Road
6.3
(unpaved road)
8
APPLEGATE 8
RUCH
Sterlingville Cemetery 1863
Applegate River
2.6
Little Applegate Road
sketch
4.4
look for mining tailings
1.5
3.1
(unpaved road)
BUNCOM (site)
cross the Applegate here at Cameron Bridge
3.2
Applegate Road
Applegate River
Little Applegate River
CRUMP (site)
sketch
McKEE BRIDGE
TO STEAMBOAT (SITE)

Buncom

# McKee Bridge to Applegate via Steamboat

Once past the Applegate Lake reservoir the road was picturesque, with meadows, streams and, near the site of Steamboat, with overhanging forest trees. Along Thompson Creek toward Applegate there were many great barns and farms in lovely pastoral settings.

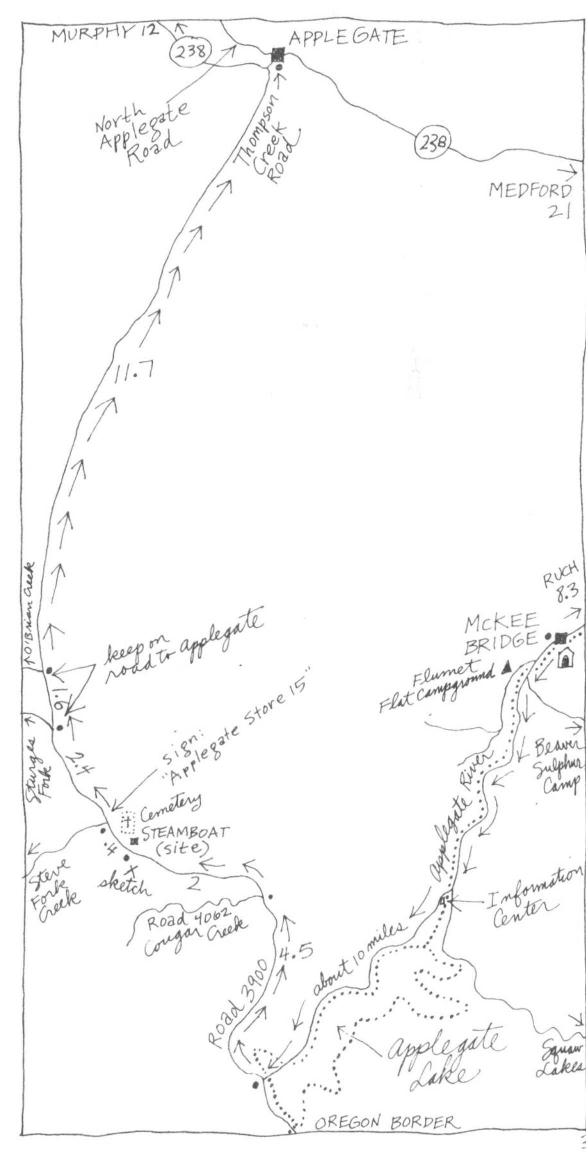
MURPHY 12
238
APPLEGATE
North Applegate Road
Thompson Creek Road
238
MEDFORD 21
11.7
O'Brian Creek
keep on road to applegate
1.6
Sturges Fork
2.4
sign: "Applegate Store 15"
Cemetery
STEAMBOAT (site)
.4
Steve Fork Creek
sketch
2
Road 4062 Cougar Creek
4.5
Road 3900
about 10 miles
Applegate Lake
OREGON BORDER
RUCH 8.3
McKEE BRIDGE
Flumet Flat Campground
Beaver Sulphur Camp
Applegate River
Information Center
Squaw Lakes

McKee covered bridge

34 *The road near Steamboat*

The Krause barn, North Applegate Road

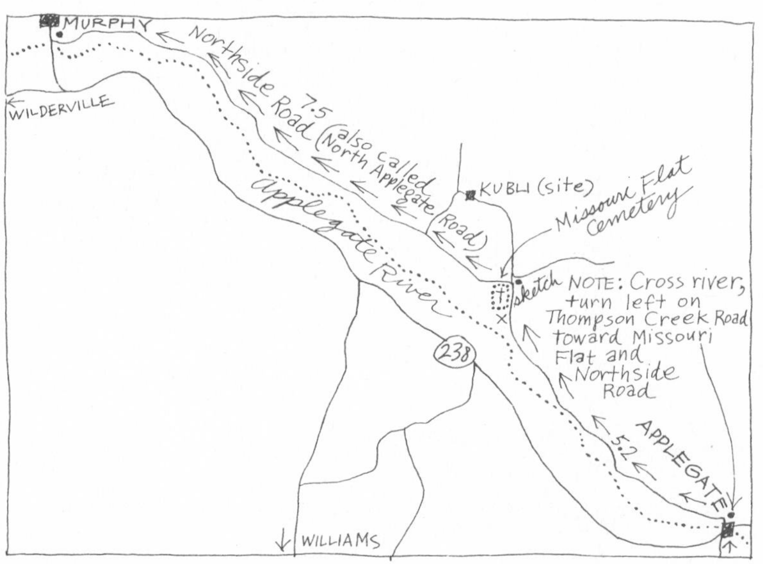

MURPHY
WILDERVILLE
Northside Road
7.5
(also called North Applegate Road)
KUBLI (site)
Missouri Flat Cemetery
sketch
NOTE: Cross river, turn left on Thompson Creek Road toward Missouri Flat and Northside Road
Applegate River
238
5.2
APPLEGATE
WILLIAMS

North Applegate Road to Murphy

This byway is also called Northside Road. It goes past meadows and barns and then idles by the Missouri Flat cemetery where "Artesian Water A Gift from God" was offered. In 1943 Bert Clute donated the water system in memory of his wife, Lydia. The good water was a gift, indeed.

## Roads to Lake of the Woods, Fourmile and Fish Lake

Dead Indian Road, off Highway 66 a mile or so south of Ashland, is scenic all the way to Lake of the Woods. Highway 140 off Highway 62 six miles north of Medford goes to Fish Lake, Lake of the Woods and past the dirt road turnoff to Fourmile Lake.

There are views of Mt. McLoughlin and I sketched the classic peak with an early morning mist mantling its base.

McLoughlin is not a popular name with old-timers in this area because he favored the British, so they say. Their name for the 9500-foot mountain was Snowy Butte, and later, Mt. Pitt.

Mount McLoughlin

# Back road to Little Lost Creek

There is a quiet back road paralleling Highway 140 through the Rogue River National Forest. It begins opposite the Big Elk Guard Station near Fish Lake. Ask about the condition of the road at the Guard Station as conditions may vary from season to season and year to year. The road eventually winds (a bit precariously) down into a green valley along the south fork of Little Butte Creek. Southeast of the tiny community of Lakecreek the road past Little Lost Creek branches off one mile to Oregon's "shortest covered bridge."

There was no traffic over the old span as I sketched. A rooster crowed, a fly bit me, green dragonflies whirred by, and spiders lowered themselves onto my drawing paper from an overhanging alder tree.

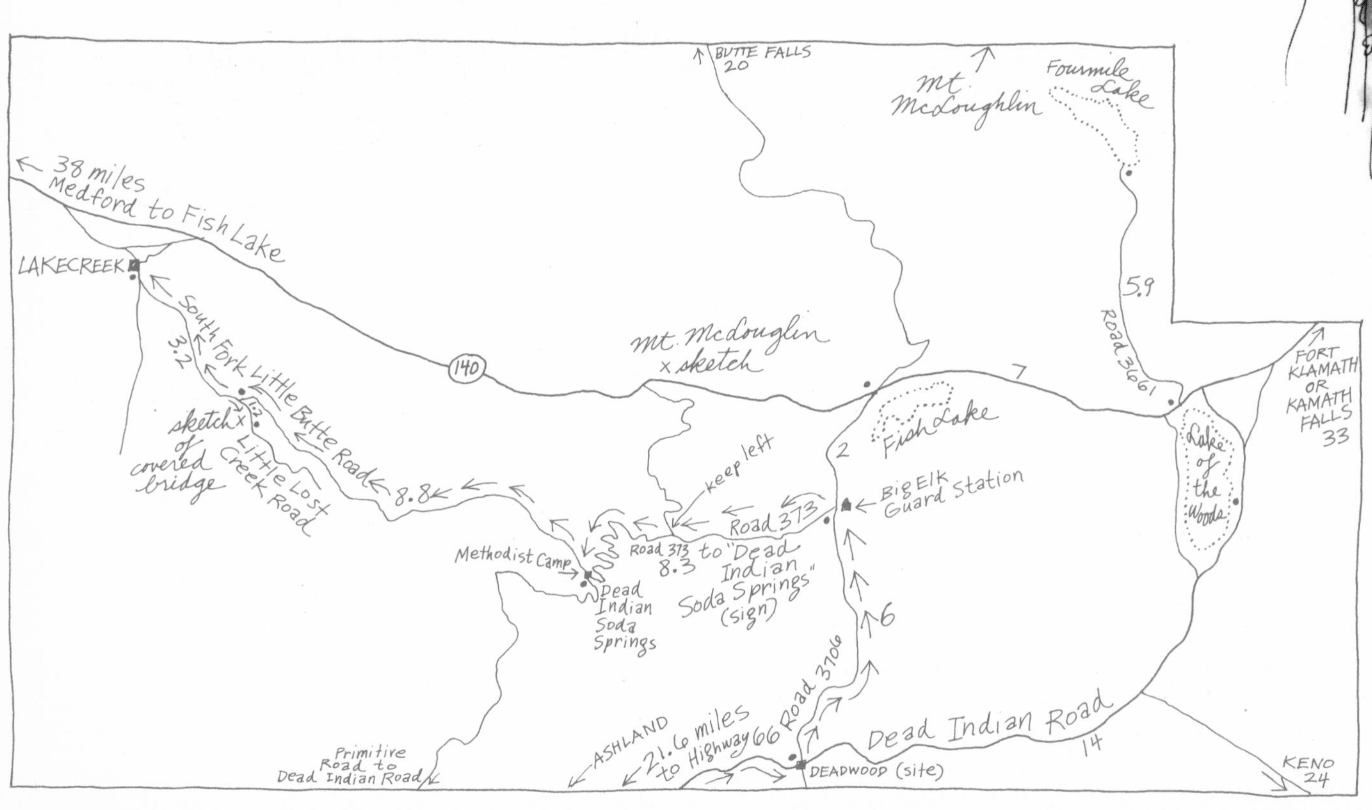

BUTTE FALLS 20
Mt. McDoughlin
Fourmile Lake
38 miles Medford to Fish Lake
LAKECREEK
South Fork Little Butte Road
3.2
sketch x of covered bridge
Little Lost Creek Road
140
Mt. McDouglin x sketch
5.9
Road 3661
7
Fish Lake
2
FORT KLAMATH OR KAMATH FALLS 33
Lake of the Woods
Keep left
8.8
Big Elk Guard Station
Road 373
Methodist Camp
Road 373 to "Dead Indian Soda Springs" (sign)
8.3
Dead Indian Soda Springs
6
Road 3706
ASHLAND
21.6 miles to Highway 66
Primitive Road to Dead Indian Road
Dead Indian Road
14
DEADWOOD (site)
KENO 24

LOAD
LIMIT
8
TONS

Little Lost Creek
Covered Bridge

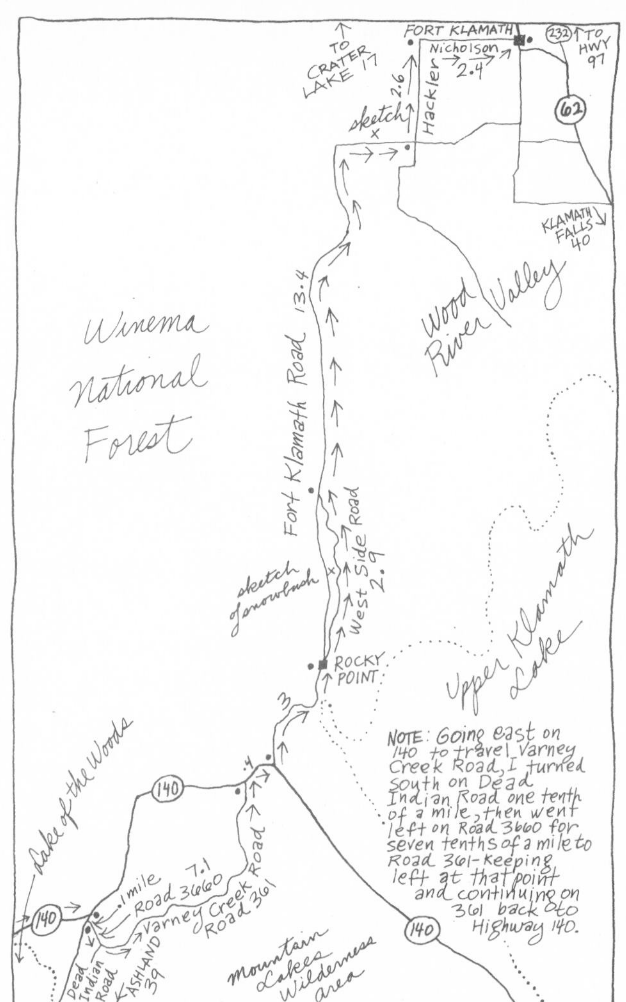
FORT KLAMATH
TO CRATER LAKE 17
2.6
Nicholson 2.4
Hacklers
232
TO HWY 97
62
sketch
KLAMATH FALLS 40
Wood River Valley
Winema National Forest
Fort Klamath Road 13.4
West Side Road 2.9
sketch of snowbush
ROCKY POINT
Upper Klamath Lake
3
.4
140
NOTE: Going east on 140 to travel Varney Creek Road, I turned south on Dead Indian Road one tenth of a mile, then went left on Road 3660 for seven tenths of a mile to Road 361-Keeping left at that point and continuing on 361 back to Highway 140.
Lake of the Woods
.1mile
7.1
Road 3660
Varney Creek Road
Road 361
Dead Indian Road
ASHLAND 39
Mountain Lakes Wilderness area

View from Klamath Meadows

## The road to Fort Klamath and the Invisible Mountain

From Lake of the Woods, Varney Creek Road parallels Highway 140, a quiet forest drive. At Rocky Point I turned off the Fort Klamath Road for the slower pace of West Side Road. In June the sweetly fragrant snowbush lined the roadside. Later, crossing Fort Klamath Meadows, I sketched the broad view looking north toward the region of Crater Lake and the now invisible Mt. Mazama, which once dominated this landscape. Indian legend tells of a great eruption and the collapse of the former 15,000-foot Mt. Mazama, a story supported by geologists.

Snowbush

# Crater Lake and Grayback Ridge Motor Nature Trail

Indian legend best describes Crater Lake to me. The medicine men of Klamath, who were the only people the Spirit Chief allowed to visit the lake, pictured it as a giant cave... "The cave is deep and bottomless, as deep and bottomless as the sky. The mountains around it sink far into the earth and reach toward the clouds. The cave is filled with blue water--water of a deeper blue than the sky which looks at itself in the lake."*

Grayback Ridge Motor Trail is through a mountain hemlock, lodgepole pine, and mixed conifer forest. On my trip chipmunks bounded across the road and fat black and gray birds, pine nut loving "Clark's Nutcrackers," were much in evidence. There were long views of Matterhornlike Union Peak, Mt. McLoughlin, Crater Peak and faraway Mt. Shasta.

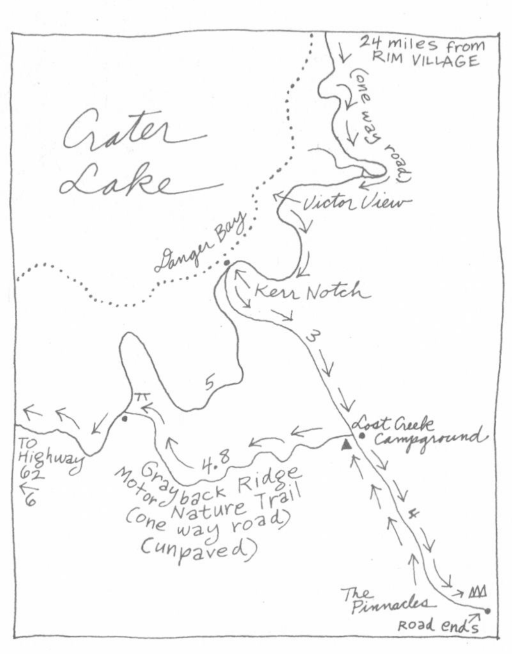
24 miles from RIM VILLAGE
(one way road)
Crater Lake
Victor View
Danger Bay
Kerr Notch
3
5
Lost Creek Campground
4.8
TO Highway 62
Grayback Ridge Motor Nature Trail (one way road) (unpaved)
4
The Pinnacles
Road ends

*from Indian Legends of the Pacific Northwest, by Ella E. Clark; Copyright 1953, The Regents of the University of California; reprinted by permission of the University of California Press.

Crater Lake

High bluffs near Toketee Falls

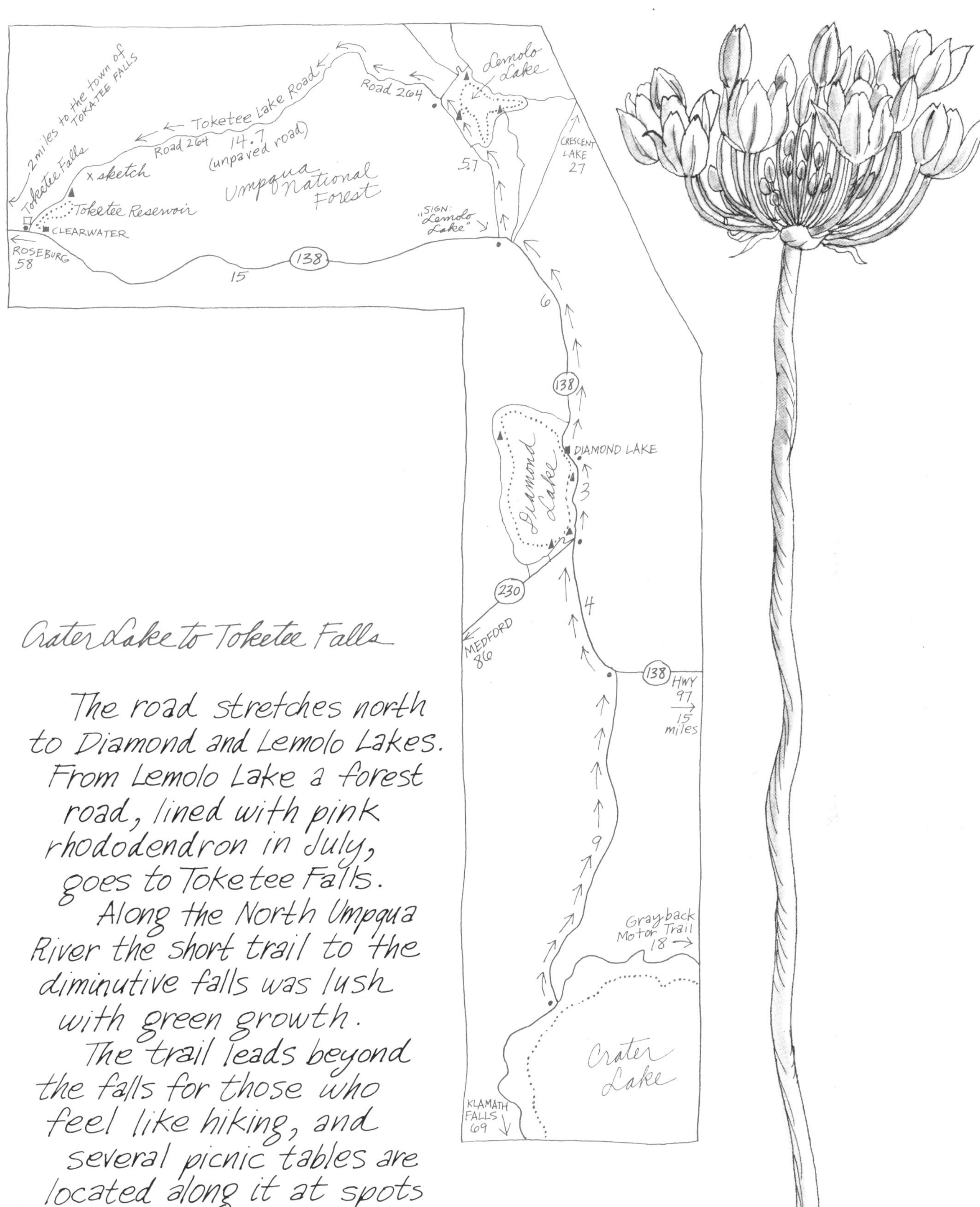
2 miles to the town of TOKATEE FALLS
Toketee Falls
x sketch
Toketee Reservoir
CLEARWATER
ROSEBURG 58
15
138
← Toketee Lake Road
Road 264
14.7
(unpaved road)
Umpqua National Forest
Road 264
Lemolo Lake
5.7
SIGN: "Lemolo Lake"
CRESCENT LAKE 27
6
138
DIAMOND LAKE
Diamond Lake
3
230
MEDFORD 86
4
138
HWY 97
15 miles
9
Grayback Motor Trail 18
Crater Lake
KLAMATH FALLS 69

# Crater Lake to Toketee Falls

The road stretches north to Diamond and Lemolo Lakes. From Lemolo Lake a forest road, lined with pink rhododendron in July, goes to Toketee Falls.

Along the North Umpqua River the short trail to the diminutive falls was lush with green growth.

The trail leads beyond the falls for those who feel like hiking, and several picnic tables are located along it at spots of infinite beauty.

Wild onion

Tiger Lily

Blackberry

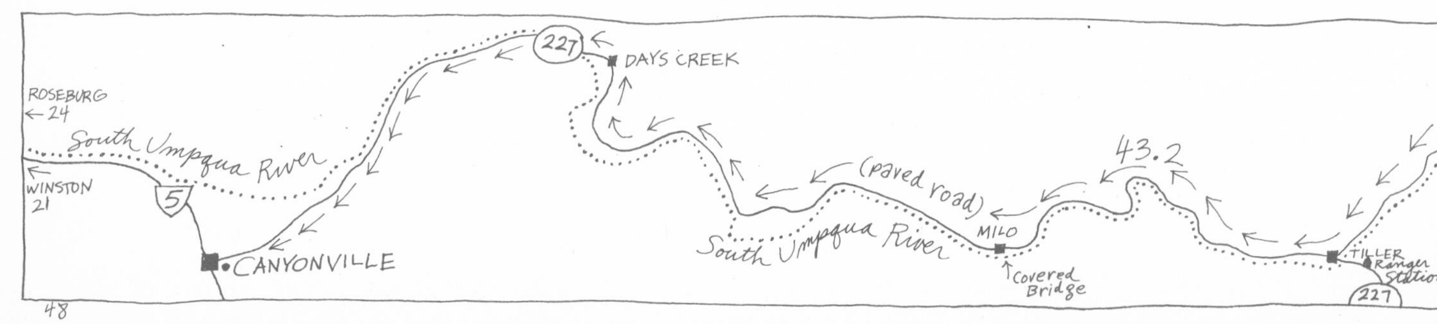

ROSEBURG
24
WINSTON
21
South Umpqua River
5
CANYONVILLE
227
DAYS CREEK
43.2
(paved road)
MILO
South Umpqua River
Covered Bridge
TILLER
Ranger Station
227

# Road to the South Umpqua River

This is a forest drive lined with yarrow, lupine, and elderberry along the roadside. I stopped to draw a brilliant orange tiger lily. At South Umpqua Falls I had a swim before sitting down to draw. Young people were diving and tumbling over the falls, and a group of boys in five truck inner tubes held onto each other as they went over the falls. I had some doubts about their safety, but in the tangle of tubes, bodies, and churning water, they survived with much shouting and laughter.

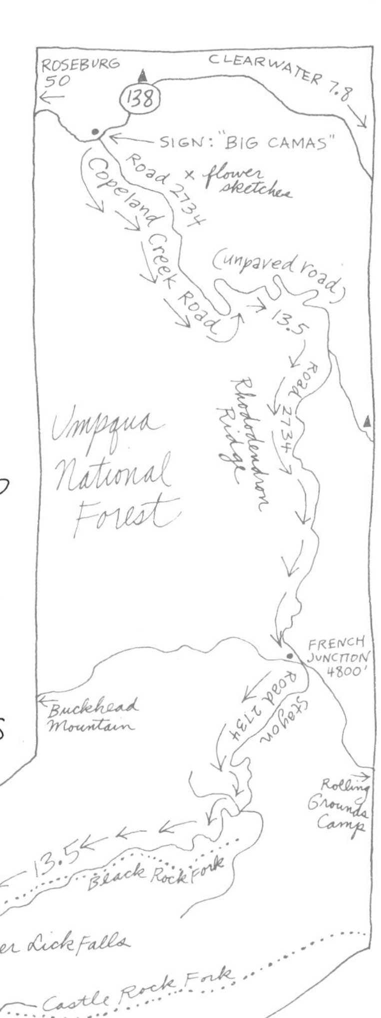

ROSEBURG 50
CLEARWATER 7.8
138
SIGN: "BIG CAMAS"
× flower sketches
Road 2734
Copeland Creek Road
(unpaved road)
13.5
Road 2734
Rhododendron Ridge
Umpqua National Forest
FRENCH JUNCTION 4800'
Buckhead Mountain
Road 2734
Rolling Grounds Camp
13.5
Black Rock Fork
Deer Lick Falls
Castle Rock Fork
Road 2734
Road 2838
4.4
South Umpqua River
× South Umpqua Falls sketch
Road 284
Campbell Falls
Umpqua National Forest
South Umpqua River

Starflower

South Umpqua Falls

Brambles in
the window

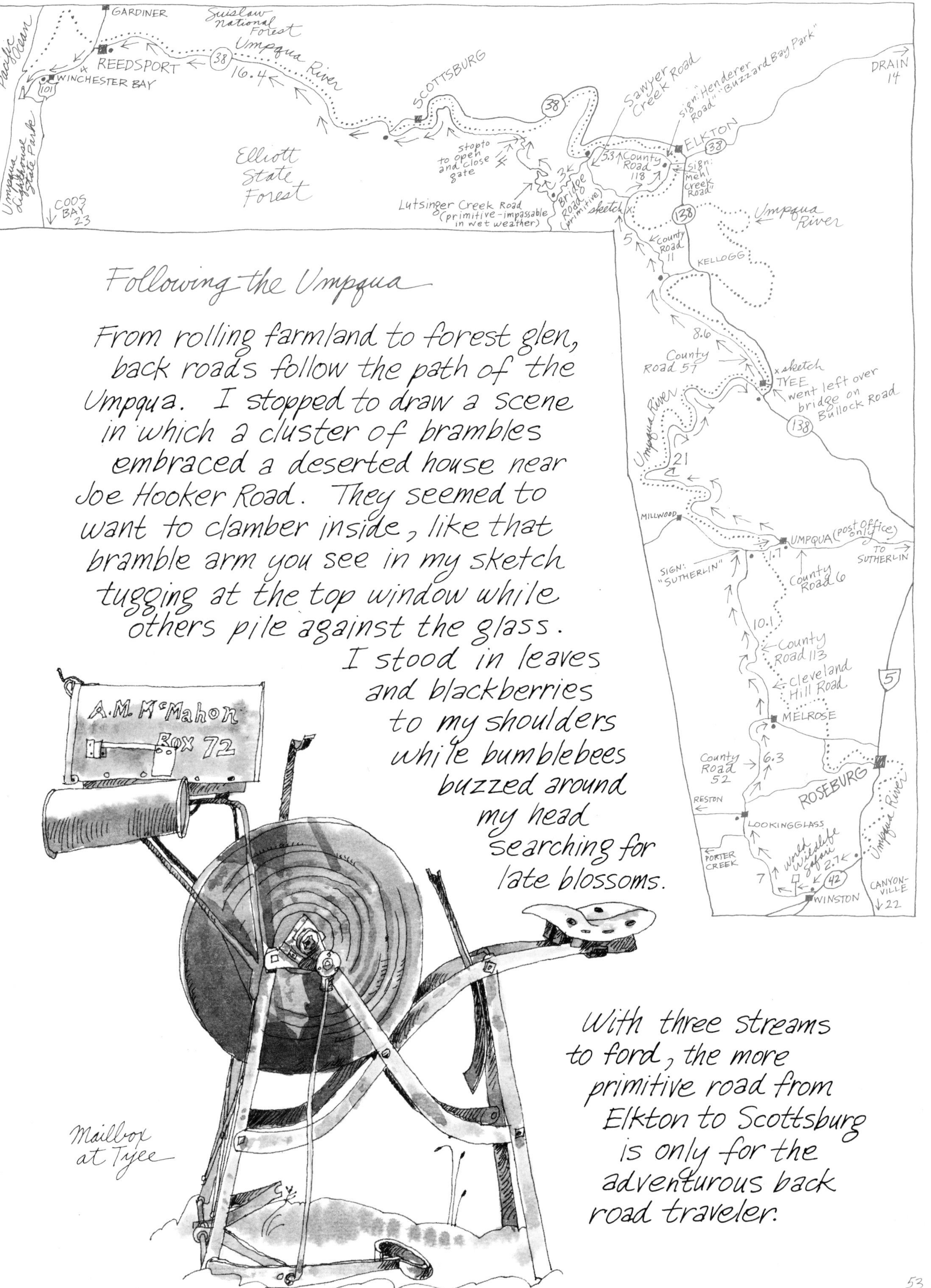
GARDINER
Siuslaw National Forest
Umpqua River
Pacific Ocean
REEDSPORT
4
38
16.4
WINCHESTER BAY
101
SCOTTSBURG
38
Sawyer Creek Road
sign: "Henderer Road" "Buzzard Bay Park"
DRAIN 14
ELKTON
38
Elliott State Forest
stop to open and close gate
3K
5.3
County Road 118
sign: "Mehl Creek Road"
Bridge Road (primitive)
Lutsinger Creek Road (primitive - impassable in wet weather)
sketch
138
Umpqua River
Umpqua Lighthouse State Park
COOS BAY 23
5
County Road 11
KELLOGG
8.6
County Road 57
x sketch
TYEE
went left over bridge on Bullock Road
138
Umpqua River
21
MILLWOOD
UMPQUA (post office only)
TO SUTHERLIN
sign: "SUTHERLIN"
1.7
County Road 6
10.1
County Road 113
Cleveland Hill Road
5
MELROSE
County Road 52
6.3
RESTON
ROSEBURG
LOOKINGGLASS
PORTER CREEK
World Wildlife Safari
2.7
Umpqua River
7
42
WINSTON
CANYONVILLE 22
A.M. McMahon
BOX 72

## Following the Umpqua

From rolling farmland to forest glen, back roads follow the path of the Umpqua. I stopped to draw a scene in which a cluster of brambles embraced a deserted house near Joe Hooker Road. They seemed to want to clamber inside, like that bramble arm you see in my sketch tugging at the top window while others pile against the glass. I stood in leaves and blackberries to my shoulders while bumblebees buzzed around my head searching for late blossoms.

Mailbox at Tyee

With three streams to ford, the more primitive road from Elkton to Scottsburg is only for the adventurous back road traveler.

COAST GUARD

## The little road to Umpqua River Lighthouse

Near Reedsport the Umpqua finally empties into the Pacific Ocean. The nicely proportioned Umpqua River Lighthouse was built in 1892, and its 1,800,000-candlepower light can be seen for twenty miles.

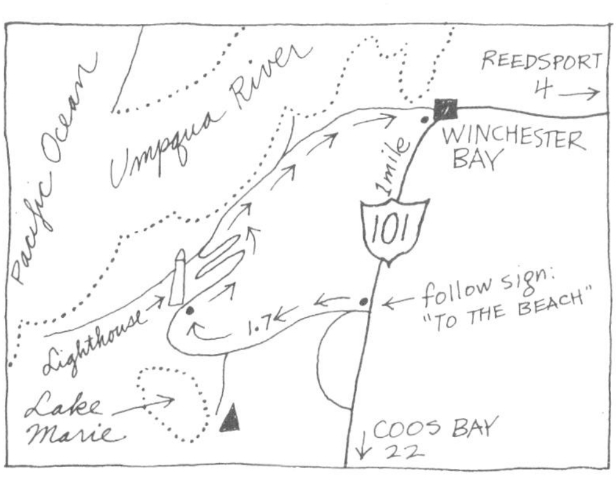
Pacific Ocean
Umpqua River
REEDSPORT
4
WINCHESTER
BAY
1 mile
101
follow sign:
"TO THE BEACH"
1.7
Lighthouse
Lake
Marie
COOS BAY
22

Umpqua River Lighthouse

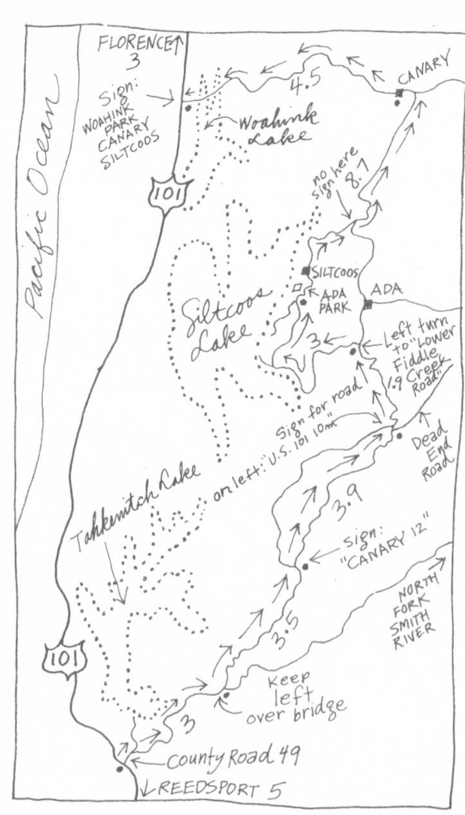
FLORENCE 3
Sign: WOAHINK PARK CANARY SILTCOOS
Woahink Lake
4.5
CANARY
Pacific Ocean
101
no sign here
8.7
SILTCOOS
ADA PARK
ADA
Siltcoos Lake
3
Left turn to "Lower Fiddle Creek Road"
1.9
Sign for road on left: "U.S. 101 10mi"
Dead End Road
Tahkenitch Lake
3.9
Sign: "CANARY 12"
NORTH FORK SMITH RIVER
3.5
101
Keep left over bridge
3
County Road 49
REEDSPORT 5

## The road to Siltcoos

Here are views of lakes and inlets filled with pond lilies, rushes, old stumps, and ancient mossy logs.

Indians called the yellow-blossomed pond lily I sketched "Wocus," and roasted and ate the large seeds--if ducks didn't get to them first! Trout prefer the cool water under the pondlilies. To fishermen, the wocus indicates that the water is likely to be too deep for wading in hip boots.

"Wocus," Indian pond lily

# The Smith River Road to Hadleyville

Green meadows and big barns border the inland riverbank. Tidy houses are tucked into narrow forest canyons on the north side of the road.

The Twin Sisters Campground, a lovely spot shaded by fir trees, was lush and verdant with ferns. After camping there for the night I sketched a decaying fir stump that nature had adorned with intricate patterns of green growth.

Birdcalls, including the deep-throated cry of the raven, echoed in the cathedral of tall trees.

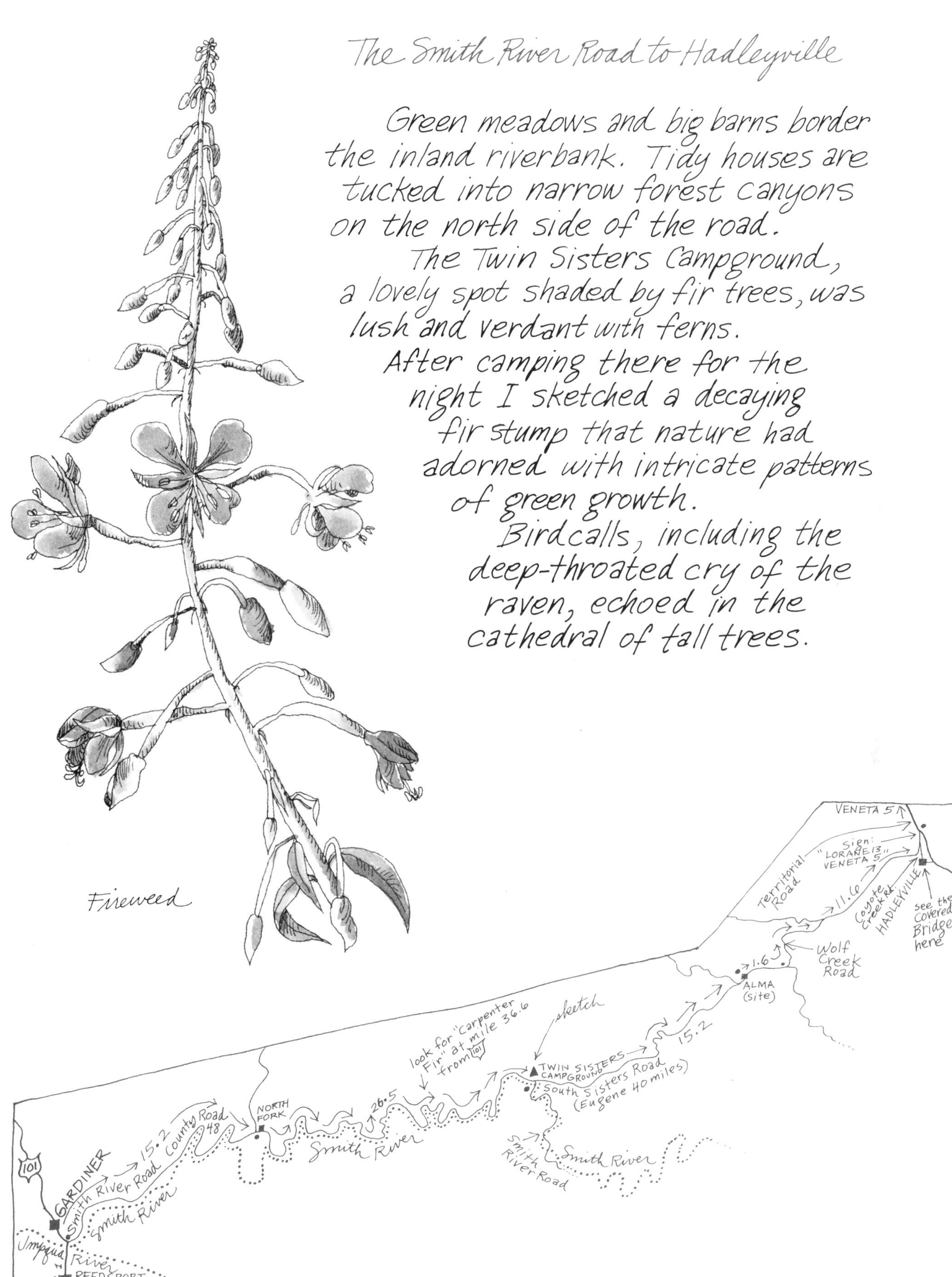

VENETA 5
Sign: "LORANE 13 VENETA 5"
Territorial Road
11.6
Coyote Creek Rd.
HADLEYVILLE
see the Covered Bridge here
Wolf Creek Road
1.6
ALMA (site)
15.2
sketch
TWIN SISTERS CAMPGROUND
South Sisters Road (Eugene 40 miles)
look for "Carpenter Fir" at mile 36.6 from 101
26.5
NORTH FORK
Smith River
Smith River Road
Smith River
Smith River Road County Road 48
15.2
GARDINER
101
Smith River
Umpqua River
REEDSPORT


Fireweed

Stump at
Twin Sisters

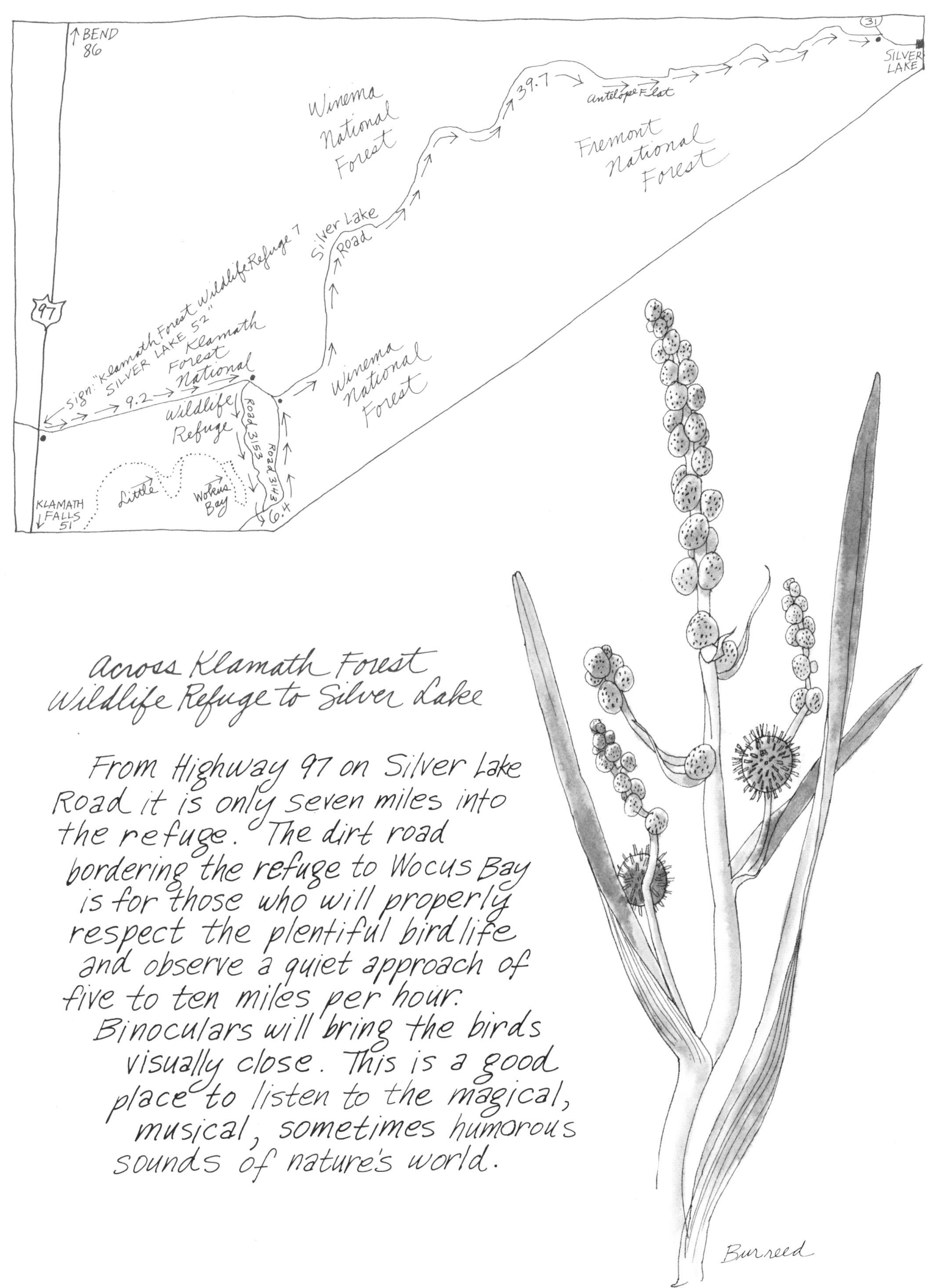
BEND
86
31
SILVER LAKE
Winema National Forest
39.7
antelope Flat
Fremont National Forest
Silver Lake Road
Sign: "Klamath Forest Wildlife Refuge 7
SILVER LAKE 52"
97
Klamath Forest National Wildlife Refuge
9.2
Winema National Forest
Road 3153
Road 3143
Little
Wokus Bay
KLAMATH FALLS 51
6.4
Burreed

## Across Klamath Forest Wildlife Refuge to Silver Lake

From Highway 97 on Silver Lake Road it is only seven miles into the refuge. The dirt road bordering the refuge to Wocus Bay is for those who will properly respect the plentiful birdlife and observe a quiet approach of five to ten miles per hour. Binoculars will bring the birds visually close. This is a good place to listen to the magical, musical, sometimes humorous sounds of nature's world.

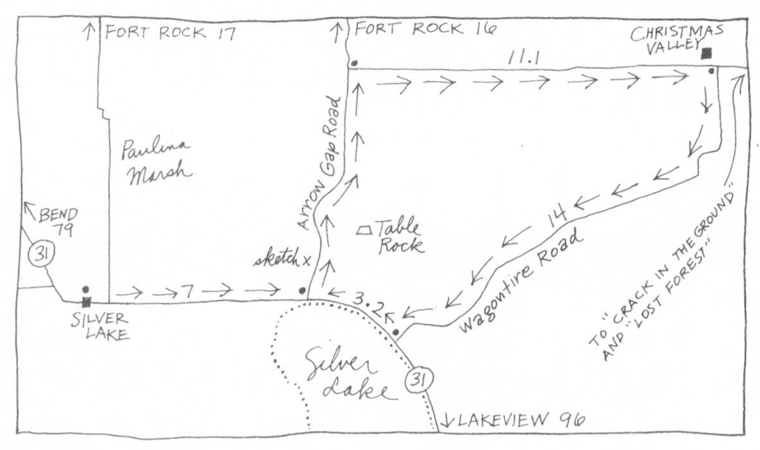
FORT ROCK 17
FORT ROCK 16
CHRISTMAS VALLEY
11.1
Paulina Marsh
Arrow Gap Road
BEND 79
31
Table Rock
sketch x
7
14
3.2
Wagontire Road
TO "CRACK IN THE GROUND" AND "LOST FOREST"
SILVER LAKE
Silver Lake
31
LAKEVIEW 96

# The road from Silver Lake

Arrow Gap Road out of Silver Lake afforded one of the many views of distinctive Table Rock. From any direction it was admirable in its proportions.

*Table Rock*

# Road to Crack-in-the-Ground

The big crack was not that easy to find, being rather poorly marked. For this reason I have made the mileage count as accurately as possible for you.

There's an interesting variation in temperature from warm to icy as you proceed to walk into the crack. In fact, the interior is so cool that early settlers used to come here for ice when everything else had melted away.

While I was sketching I was startled by a sudden fluttering of wings, and a Red-Shafted-Flicker zoomed through the crack, swerving as he narrowly missed my head.

A bit farther on this road you will see lava deposits. Then it is best to return the way you came. I went around the lava flow through miles and miles of sagebrush only generally knowing where I was. With a deteriorating passageway ahead, by luck I was able to find my way back to Christmas Valley.

miles and miles of sagebrush

*Crack-in-the-Ground*

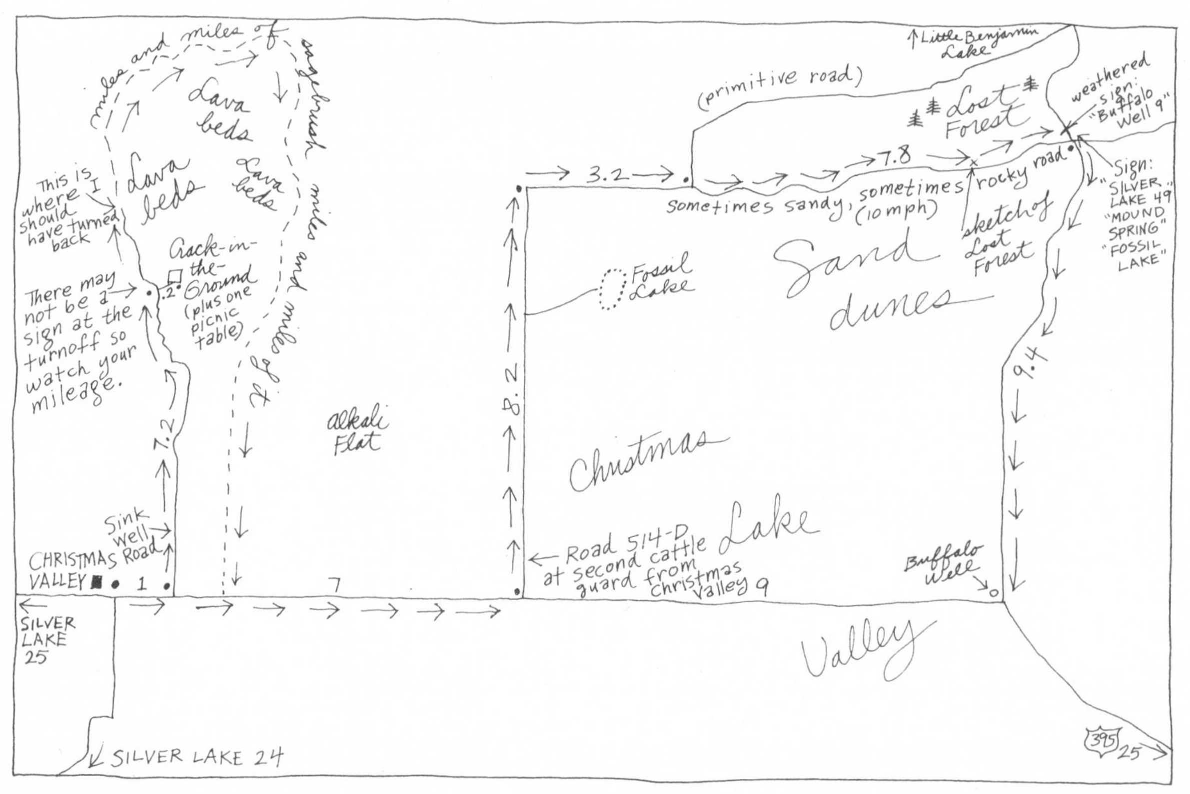

miles and miles of sagebrush miles and miles of it
Lava beds
Lava beds
Lava beds
This is where I should have turned back
Crack-in-the-Ground (plus one picnic table)
.2
There may not be a sign at the turnoff so watch your mileage.
7.2
Sink Well Road
CHRISTMAS VALLEY
1
7
SILVER LAKE 25
SILVER LAKE 24
Alkali Flat
8.2
Road 514-D at second cattle guard from Christmas Valley 9
Christmas Lake
Valley
Fossil Lake
Sand dunes
3.2
7.8
(primitive road)
Little Benjamin Lake
Lost Forest
weathered sign: "Buffalo Well 9"
Sign: "SILVER LAKE 49" "MOUND SPRING" "FOSSIL LAKE"
Sometimes sandy, sometimes rocky road (10 mph)
sketch of Lost Forest
9.4
Buffalo Well
395
25

The Lost Forest

## Through the Lost Forest

This is a primitive road and a bit far from civilization. The trip goes past Fossil Lake, where important fossils were found in the late 1800s. The Lost Forest is a unique stand of ponderosa pine growing forty miles from other forests in an area so dry that the trees only receive one-half the rainfall that they would normally need. Some of the largest junipers in Oregon also grow here.

## Back road from Fort Rock to Hole-in-the-Ground

Fort Rock really is fortresslike, and it is possible to take a somewhat precarious rim drive within the rock's interior. To the west of the rock is a butte enclosing a cave where an archeologist discovered ancient Indian sandals. These were radio-carbon dated at more than 10,000 years, making them the oldest evidence of human habitation in Oregon.

Hole-in-the-Ground, one mile wide, 300 feet deep, was formed by a violent volcanic eruption. The pattern of sagebrush and trees within the hole is striking to contemplate.

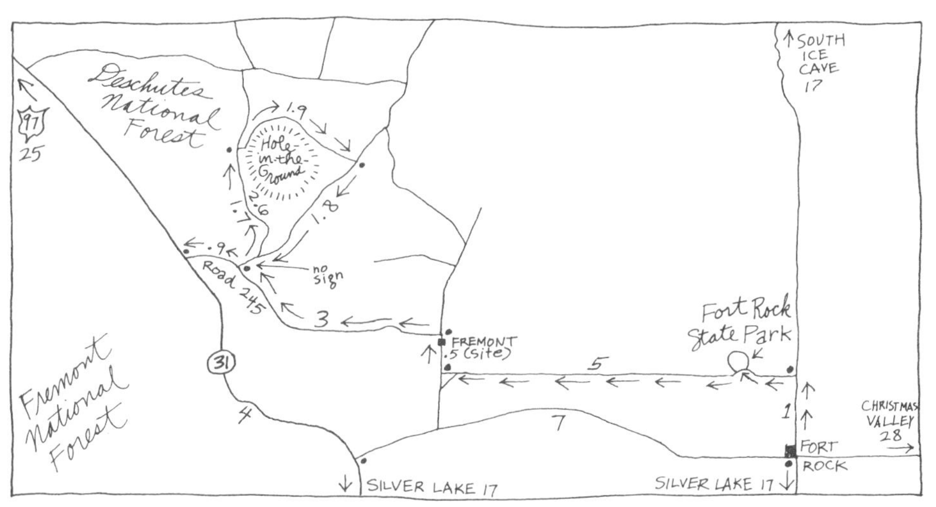
SOUTH ICE CAVE 17
Deschutes National Forest
97
25
1.9
Hole-in-the-Ground
2.6
1.7
1.8
.9
no sign
Road 245
3
Fort Rock State Park
FREMONT
.5 (site)
5
31
Fremont National Forest
4
7
1
CHRISTMAS VALLEY 28
FORT ROCK
SILVER LAKE 17
SILVER LAKE 17

Fort Rock

## Paisley to Lakeview

In Paisley I sketched the 100-year-old Tucker place, where Ma Cary, who lived there, kept a large vegetable garden. Flowers were blooming all around the little wooden house.

The old Tucker place

*Old settler's cabin in the meadow*

There were two roads from Paisley into Fremont National Forest. On the high road, in an alpine meadow near Puppy Dog Springs, was this old structure surrounded by grass and wildflowers. On a sunny day in June, when the birds are in strong and sweet voice, it is as good a place to be as anywhere on earth.

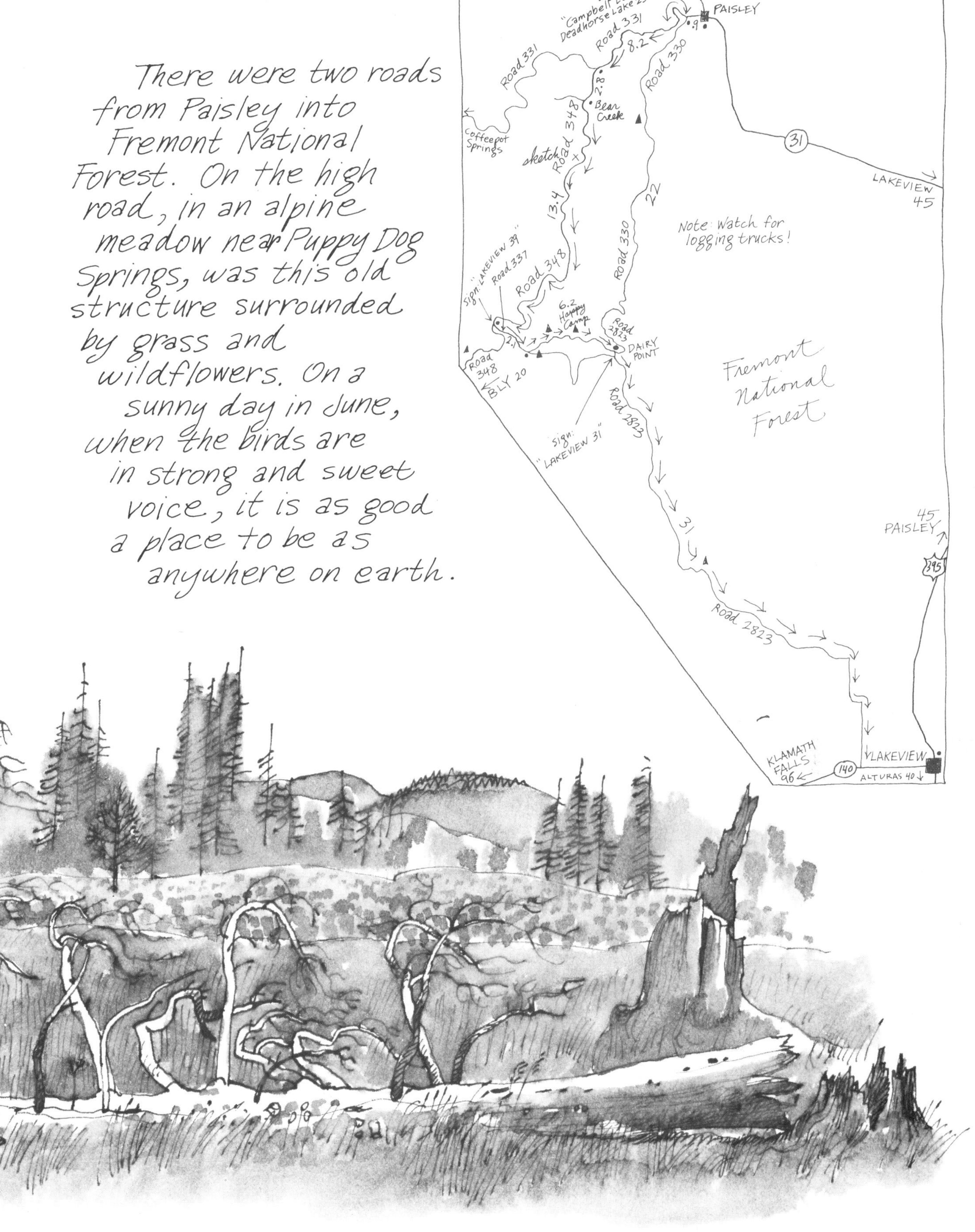
SILVER LAKE 50
PAISLEY
Sign: "Campbell Lake 22
Deadhorse Lake 23"
Road 331
.9
8.2
Road 331
Road 330
2.8
Bear Creek
Coffeepot Springs
Road 348
sketch
31
LAKEVIEW 45
13.4
22
Note: Watch for logging trucks!
Sign: "LAKEVIEW 39"
Road 337
Road 348
Road 330
6.2
Happy Camp
Road 2823
2.1
DAIRY POINT
Road 348
BLY 20
Fremont National Forest
Road 2823
Sign: "LAKEVIEW 31"
31
45 PAISLEY
395
Road 2823
KLAMATH FALLS 96
140
LAKEVIEW
ALTURAS 40

Juniper

# Dog Lake Road to Bly

I must have stayed at Dog Lake's Cinder Hill Camp on the wrong night of the week. The mosquitoes were particularly voracious. However, an old fisherman told me the fishing was good. He had a freezer in his trailer and already had a good stock of fish packed away. Along this forest road I sketched a juniper and a big mule-ears blossom. There were thousands of white pond buttercups on the pond surface at Robinson Spring. A black duck paddled through all the whiteness. I dripped a blob of black ink on my drawing while striking at a mosquito.

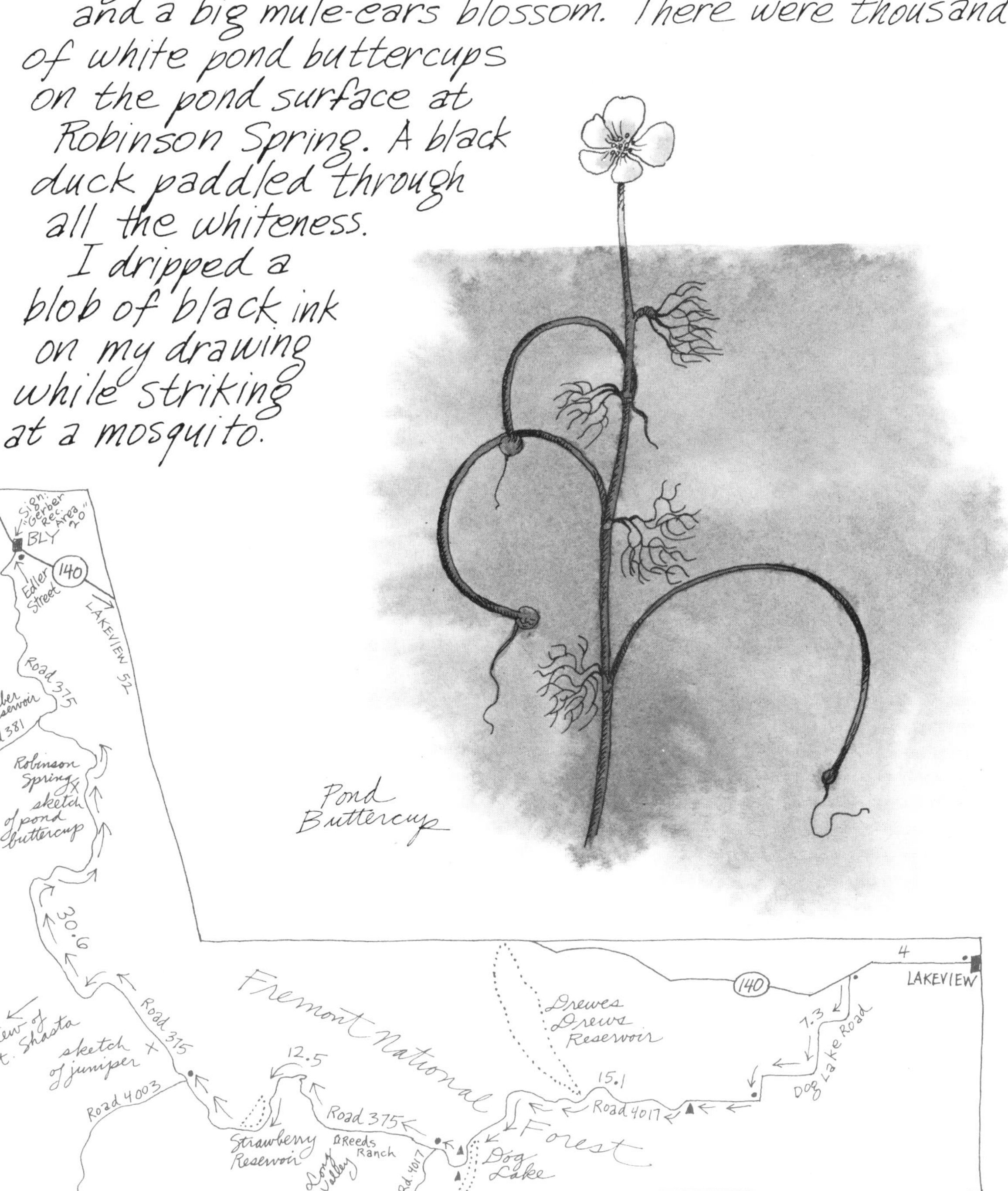
Pond Buttercup
Sign: "Gerber Rec. Area 20"
BLY
KLAMATH FALLS 54
140
Edler Street
LAKEVIEW 52
Road 375
Gerber Reservoir
Road 381
Robinson Spring
sketch of pond buttercup
30.6
Fremont National Forest
Drewes Drews Reservoir
140
4
LAKEVIEW
7.3
Dog Lake Road
15.1
Road 4017
View of Mt. Shasta
sketch of juniper
Road 375
12.5
Road 4003
Road 375
Strawberry Reservoir
Reeds Ranch
Long Valley
Rd. 4017
Dog Lake

The old Fitzhugh place,
Langell Valley

# Langell Valley Road

In Langell Valley there existed a land of old barns and sweet clover.

A loop trip with a picnic in Bonanza town's charming little park was delightful.

One-half mile west of Lorella I sketched the old Fitzhugh place (1900) in its setting of green grass and poplars.

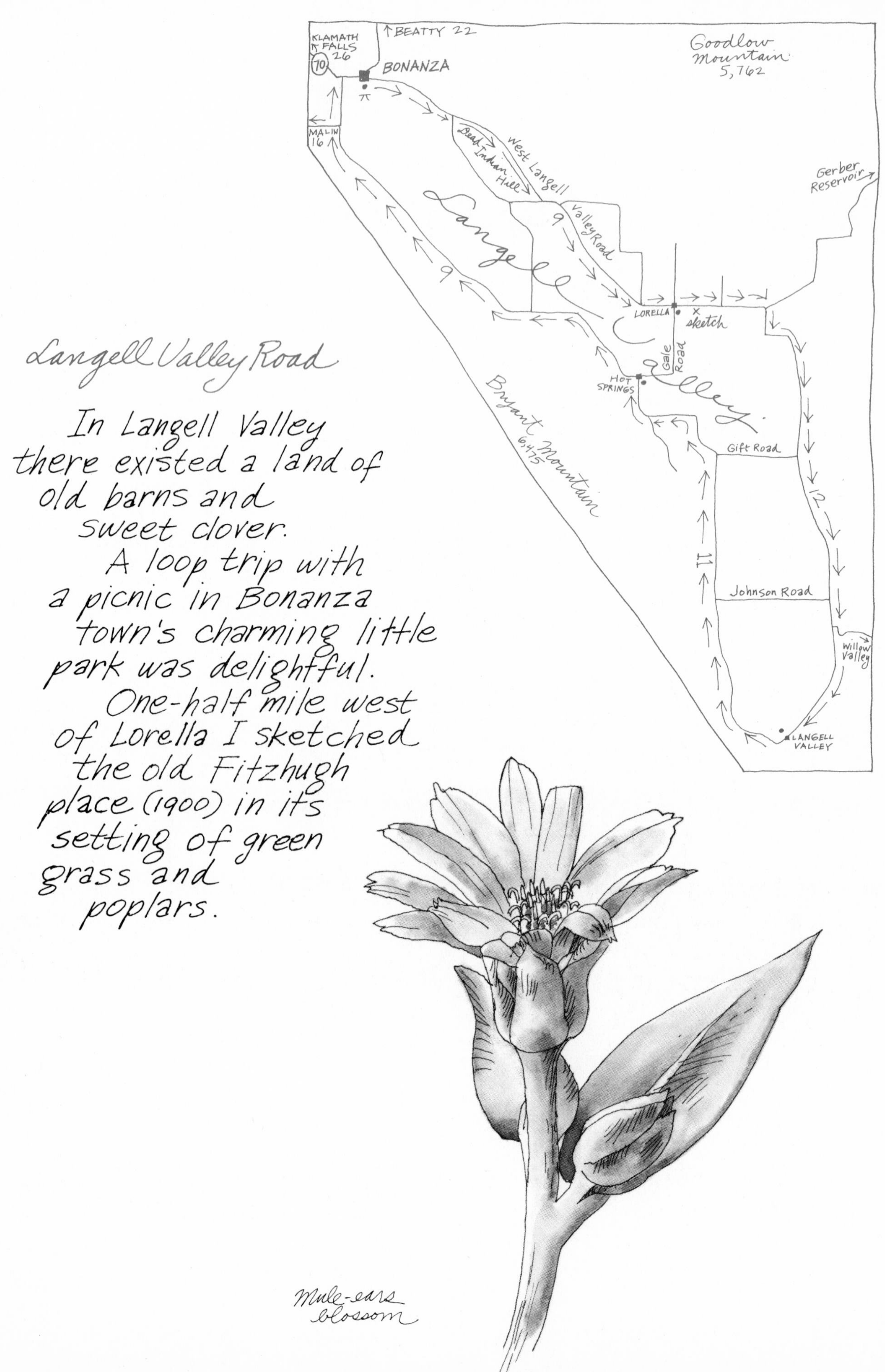

BEATTY 22
KLAMATH FALLS 26
70
BONANZA
Goodlow Mountain 5,762
MALIN 16
Dead Indian Hill
West Langell
Gerber Reservoir
Langell Valley
9
Valley Road
LORELLA
x sketch
Gale Road
HOT SPRINGS
Bryant Mountain 6,475
Gift Road
12
11
Johnson Road
Willow Valley
LANGELL VALLEY


Mule-ears blossom

## Round trip through Klamath Basin

There is much drama and many interesting sights along the canals and waterways south of Klamath Falls. Egrets were stationed at intervals along Klamath Strait Drain Outlet, each rising to flight as I traveled slowly down the levee road. Groups of cormorants flew between the dikes, geese scurried to the water to swim to the other side, hawks lay in wait to capture ducklings, and a great white pelican took off into the wind, pushing at the water surface for takeoff speed.

Typical comments by visitors in the Refuge Visitor Register were "Beyond fantastic," "Praise the Lord," "Avocet sounds are super," and my own notation, "Hooray for the birds."

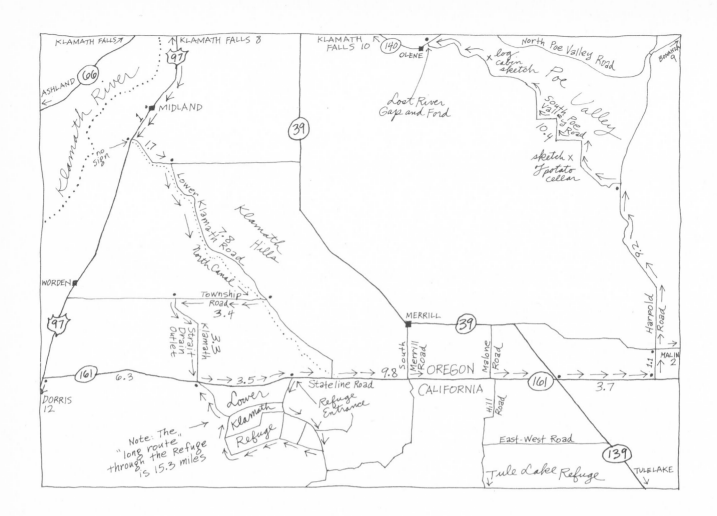

KLAMATH FALLS
KLAMATH FALLS 8
97
66
ASHLAND
Klamath River
MIDLAND
1
no sign
1.7
Lower Klamath Road
7.8
North Canal
Klamath Hills
WORDEN
Township Road
3.4
3.3
Klamath
Strait Drain Outlet
97
161
6.3
3.5
DORRIS 12
Stateline Road
Refuge Entrance
Lower Klamath Refuge
Note: The "long route" through the Refuge is 15.3 miles
KLAMATH FALLS 10
140
OLENE
Lost River Gap and Ford
39
x log cabin sketch
North Poe Valley Road
Poe Valley
BONANZA 9
South Poe Valley Road
10.4
sketch x potato cellar
9.2
Harpold Road
MERRILL
39
South Merrill Road
9.8
OREGON
CALIFORNIA
Malone Road
Hill Road
161
3.7
1.1
MALIN 2
East-West Road
139
Tule Lake Refuge
TULELAKE

Potato Cellar

Within Poe Valley, and indeed in all the farming country hereabouts, are potato cellars. Farmers can store potatoes in these insulated half-barns from September to April.

I drew the trapper's cabin on the site of a Modoc Indian campground. Sam High originally purchased the land from the first homesteader in about 1880. Sam High's grandson told me the cabin is known to have been there in 1860.

In returning to Highway 140 on this round trip through Klamath Basin, a bridge crosses the Lost River fording place used by the earliest travelers in this section of Oregon.

*Trapper's cabin, circa 1860*

# The road from Westfir to Lowell

There are four covered bridges in the Lowell area, the most picturesque setting being at Unity.

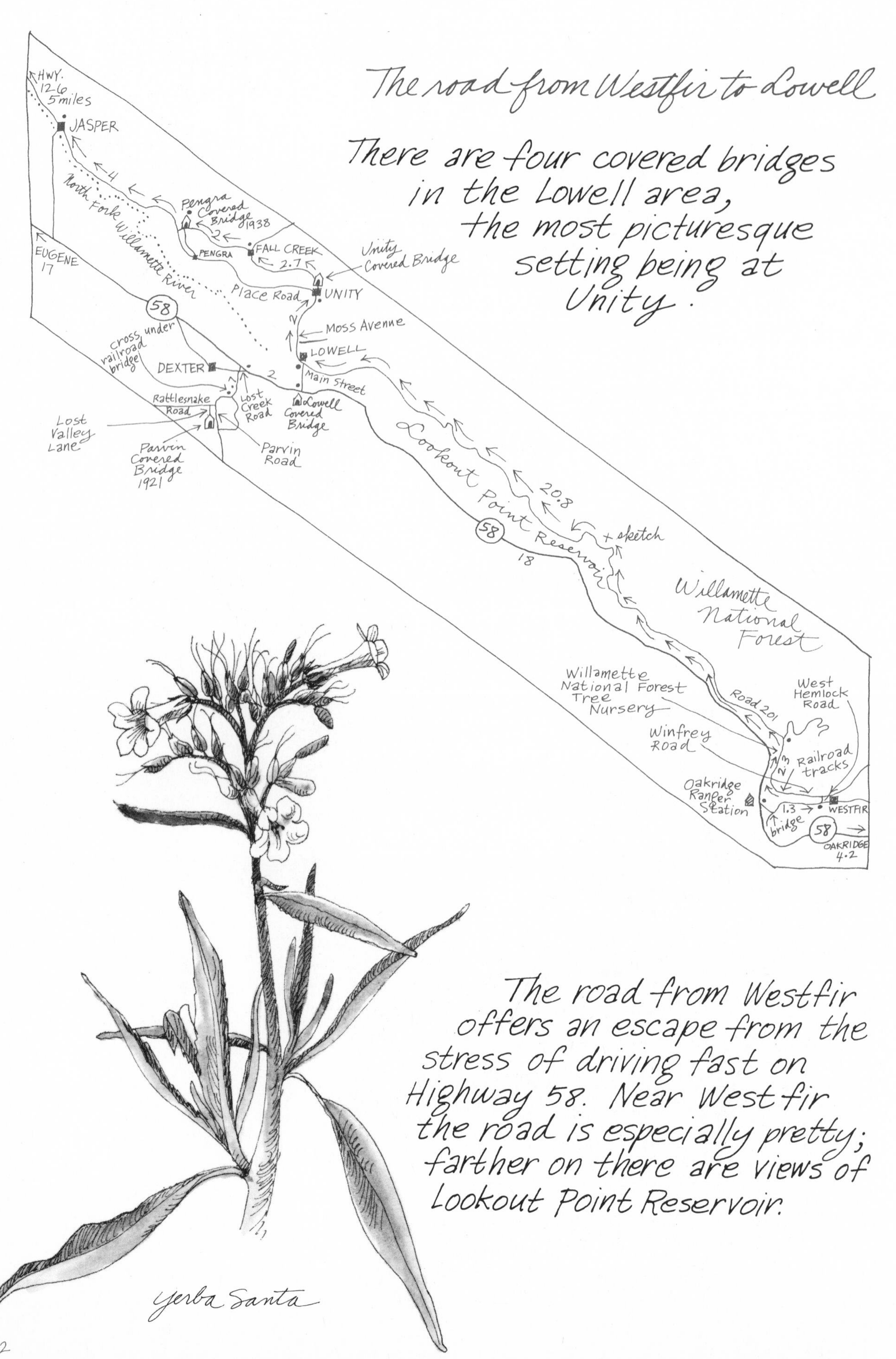
HWY. 126 5 miles
JASPER
4
North Fork Willamette River
Pengra Covered Bridge 1938
2
PENGRA
FALL CREEK
2.7
Unity Covered Bridge
UNITY
Place Road
EUGENE 17
58
Moss Avenue
LOWELL
cross under railroad bridge
DEXTER
2
Main Street
Lost Creek Road
Lowell Covered Bridge
Rattlesnake Road
Lost Valley Lane
Parvin Covered Bridge 1921
Parvin Road
Lookout Point Reservoir
20.8
+ sketch
58
18
Willamette National Forest
Willamette National Forest Tree Nursery
Road 201
West Hemlock Road
Winfrey Road
Railroad tracks
Oakridge Ranger Station
1.3
bridge
WESTFIR
58
OAKRIDGE 4.2

The road from Westfir offers an escape from the stress of driving fast on Highway 58. Near Westfir the road is especially pretty; farther on there are views of Lookout Point Reservoir.

Yerba Santa

The road from Westfir

## Back road of caves and lakes

The landscape was of pine and sagebrush, gently rolling across the high desert.
At Skeleton Cave I sketched by flashlight in the cool interior.
There was much to see in this volcanic area south of Bend.
With stops at four caves, this back road took me to Newberry Crater and its two popular fishing lakes, East and Paulina. Then there was Lava Cast Forest, Lava River Caves, and Lava Butte to visit on the way back to Bend.

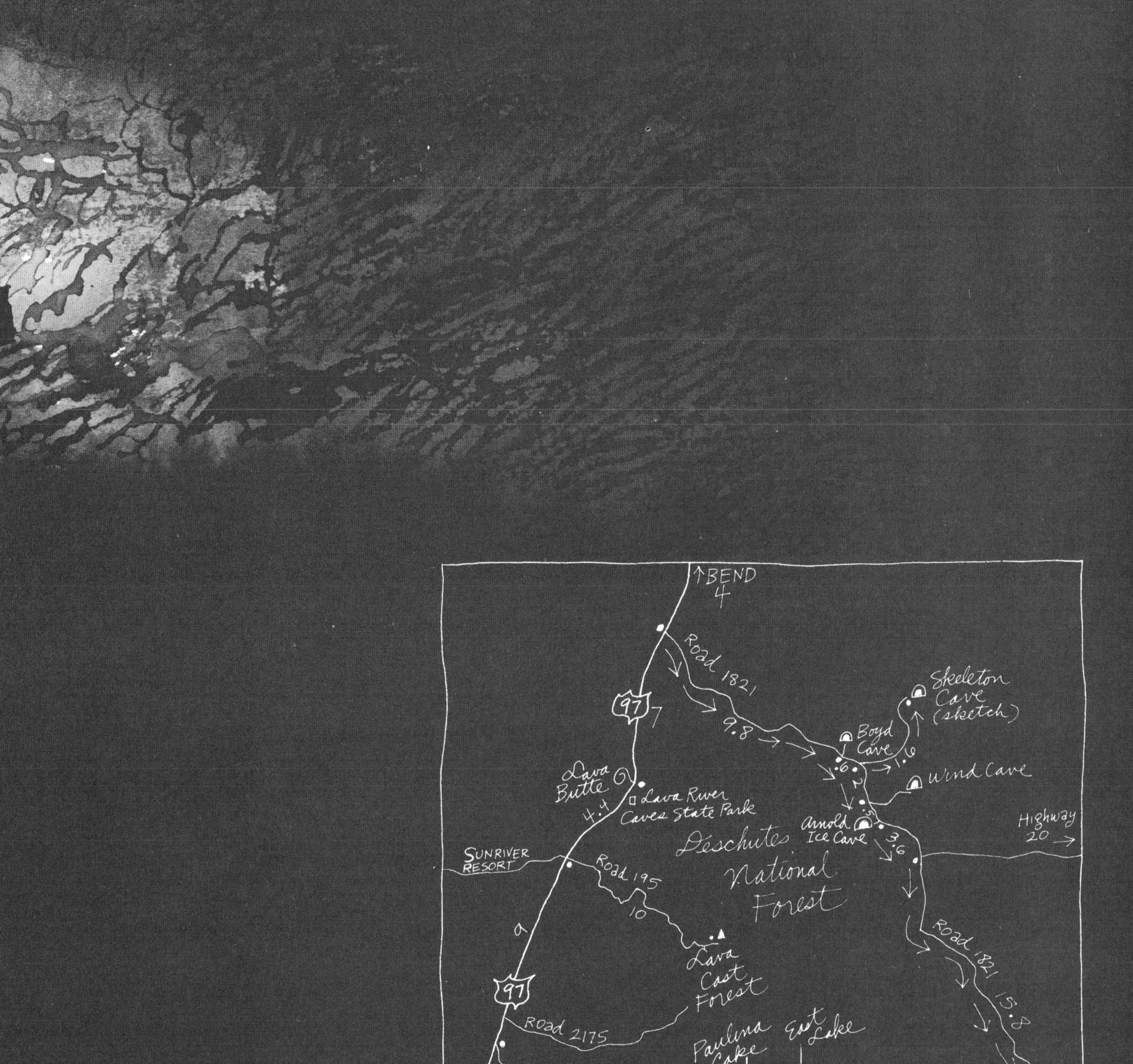

BEND
4
Road 1821
97
7
9.8
Skeleton Cave (sketch)
Boyd Cave
.6
1.6
Wind Cave
Lava Butte
Lava River Caves State Park
4.4
Arnold Ice Cave
Highway 20
3.6
SUNRIVER RESORT
Road 195
Deschutes National Forest
10
9
Lava Cast Forest
97
Road 1821
15.8
Road 2175
Paulina Lake
East Lake
14
4
10
Paulina Peak 7984'
Road 2129
CHINA HAT
3

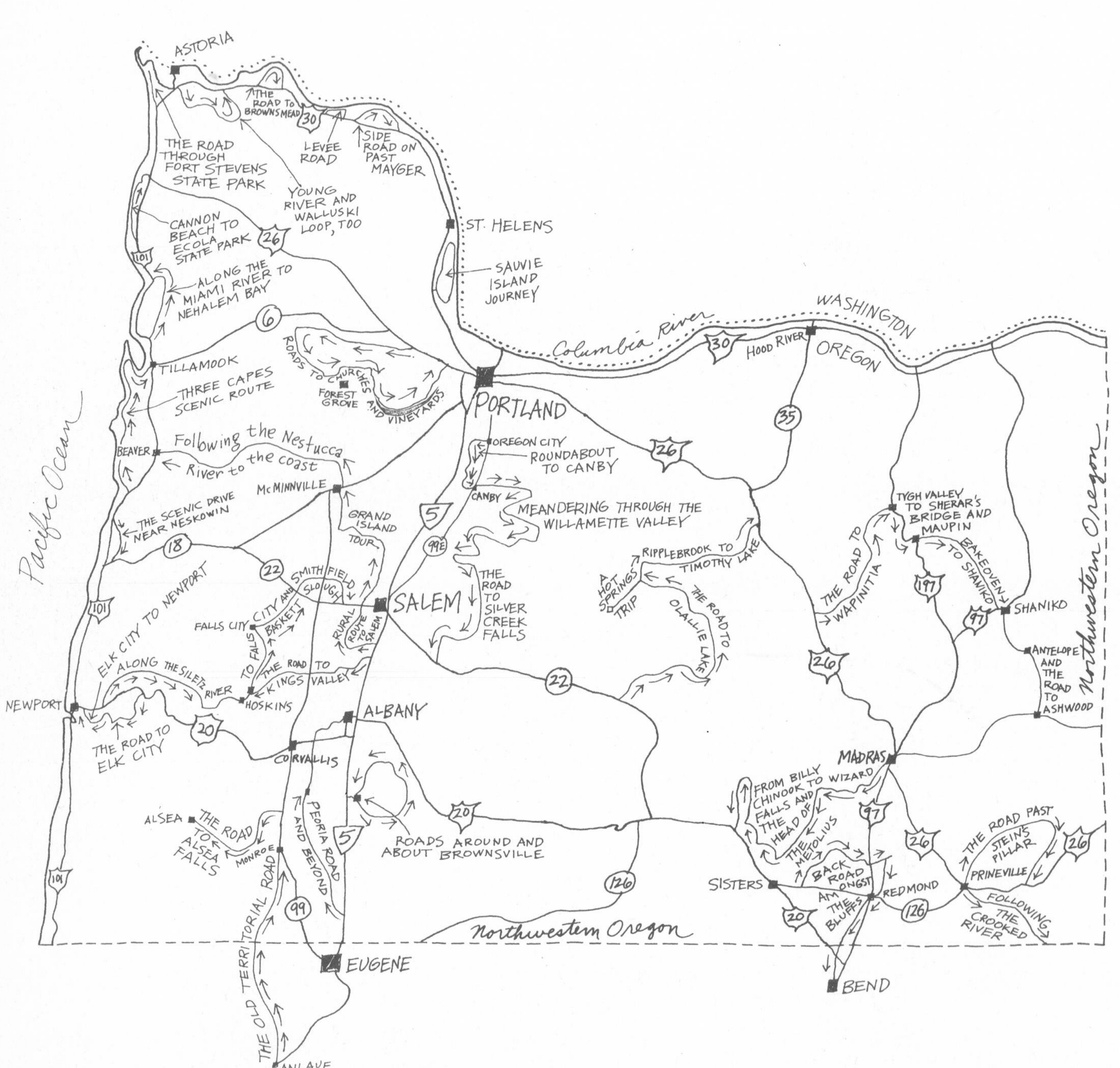
ASTORIA
THE ROAD TO BROWNSMEAD
LEVEE ROAD
SIDE ROAD ON PAST MAYGER
THE ROAD THROUGH FORT STEVENS STATE PARK
YOUNG RIVER AND WALLUSKI LOOP, TOO
CANNON BEACH TO ECOLA STATE PARK
ST. HELENS
SAUVIE ISLAND JOURNEY
ALONG THE MIAMI RIVER TO NEHALEM BAY
WASHINGTON
Columbia River
HOOD RIVER
OREGON
TILLAMOOK
ROADS TO CHURCHES AND VINEYARDS
FOREST GROVE
THREE CAPES SCENIC ROUTE
PORTLAND
Pacific Ocean
BEAVER
Following the Nestucca River to the coast
OREGON CITY
ROUNDABOUT TO CANBY
McMINNVILLE
CANBY
MEANDERING THROUGH THE WILLAMETTE VALLEY
GRAND ISLAND TOUR
THE SCENIC DRIVE NEAR NESKOWIN
TYGH VALLEY TO SHERAR'S BRIDGE AND MAUPIN
BAKEOVEN TO SHANIKO
SMITHFIELD SLOUGH
RIPPLEBROOK TO TIMOTHY LAKE
A HOT SPRINGS TRIP
THE ROAD TO WAPINITIA
THE ROAD TO SILVER CREEK FALLS
SALEM
THE ROAD TO OLALLIE LAKE
SHANIKO
ELK CITY TO NEWPORT
FALLS CITY
TO FALLS CITY AND BASKETT
RURAL ROUTE TO SALEM
ANTELOPE AND THE ROAD TO ASHWOOD
Northwestern Oregon
ALONG THE SILETZ RIVER
THE ROAD TO KINGS VALLEY
HOSKINS
NEWPORT
ALBANY
THE ROAD TO ELK CITY
CORVALLIS
MADRAS
FROM BILLY CHINOOK FALLS AND THE HEAD OF THE METOLIUS TO WIZARD
ALSEA
THE ROAD TO ALSEA FALLS
MONROE
PEORIA ROAD AND BEYOND
ROADS AROUND AND ABOUT BROWNSVILLE
THE ROAD PAST STEIN'S PILLAR
BACK ROAD AMONGST THE BLUFFS
PRINEVILLE
SISTERS
REDMOND
FOLLOWING THE CROOKED RIVER
Northwestern Oregon
EUGENE
BEND
THE OLD TERRITORIAL ROAD
ANLAUF
30
26
101
6
35
5
99E
18
22
97
197
20
126
99

Foxglove

# Northwestern Oregon

This is a land of enchanting Pacific shoreline, lush green coastal forest, great snowcapped inland mountains, majestic rivers and fertile valleys, and high desert land textured with sagebrush and juniper.

# The old Territorial Road

You can travel the old stage road from Anlauf north to Monroe. Along Pheasant Creek it twists and turns as the original road probably did long ago. Farther north it has been smoothed and straightened into a fast highway.

Near Franklin I sketched the Allen barn, erected in 1900, two years before the house was built. A chipmunk sat gnawing an acorn just a few yards from my feet. I included it in the picture.

The allen barn, 1900

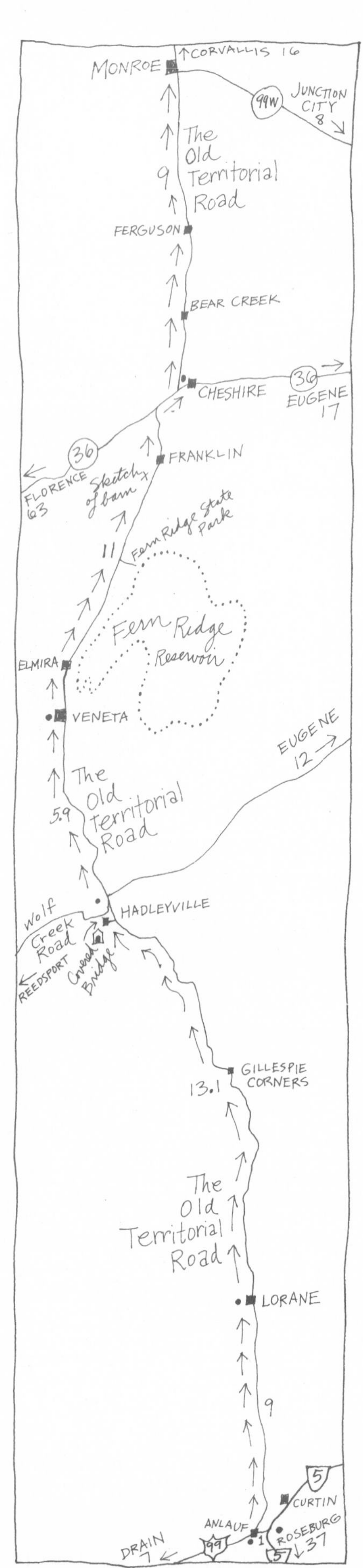
MONROE
CORVALLIS 16
99W
JUNCTION CITY 8
9
The Old Territorial Road
FERGUSON
BEAR CREEK
CHESHIRE
36
EUGENE 17
36
FLORENCE 63
FRANKLIN
Sketch of barn
11
Fern Ridge State Park
Fern Ridge Reservoir
ELMIRA
VENETA
EUGENE 12
5.9
The Old territorial Road
Wolf Creek Road
HADLEYVILLE
REEDSPORT
Covered Bridge
GILLESPIE CORNERS
13.1
The Old Territorial Road
LORANE
9
5
CURTIN
ANLAUF
1
ROSEBURG 37
DRAIN 7
99
5

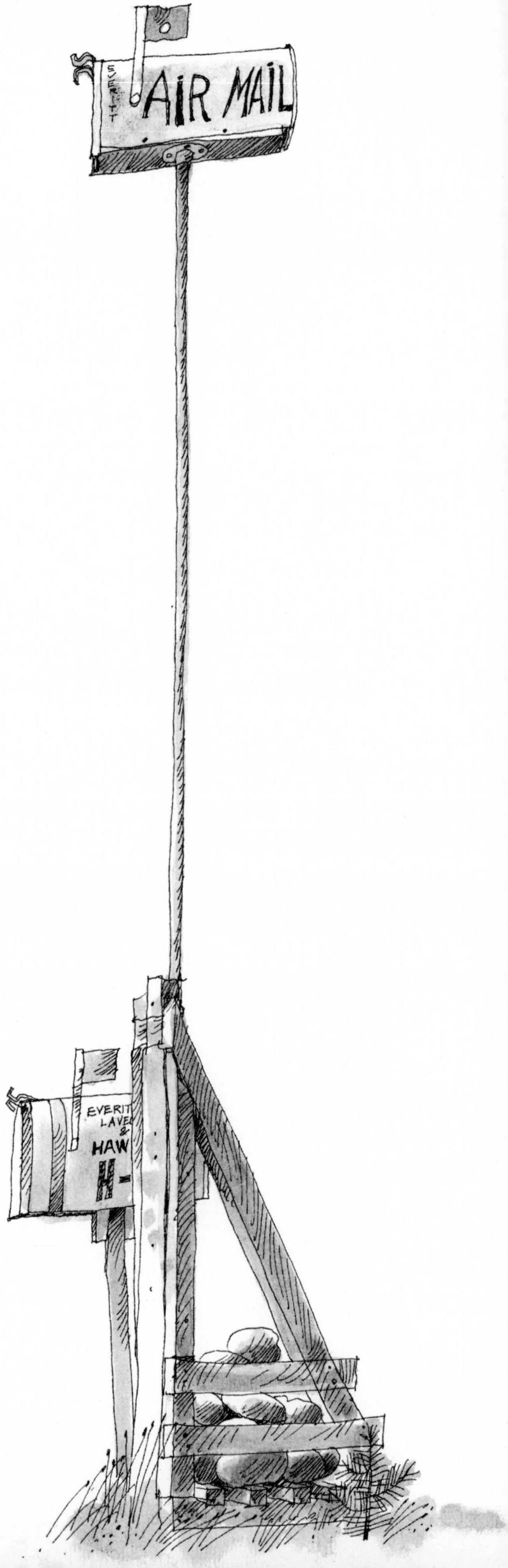

Back road airmail

Back road mailbox

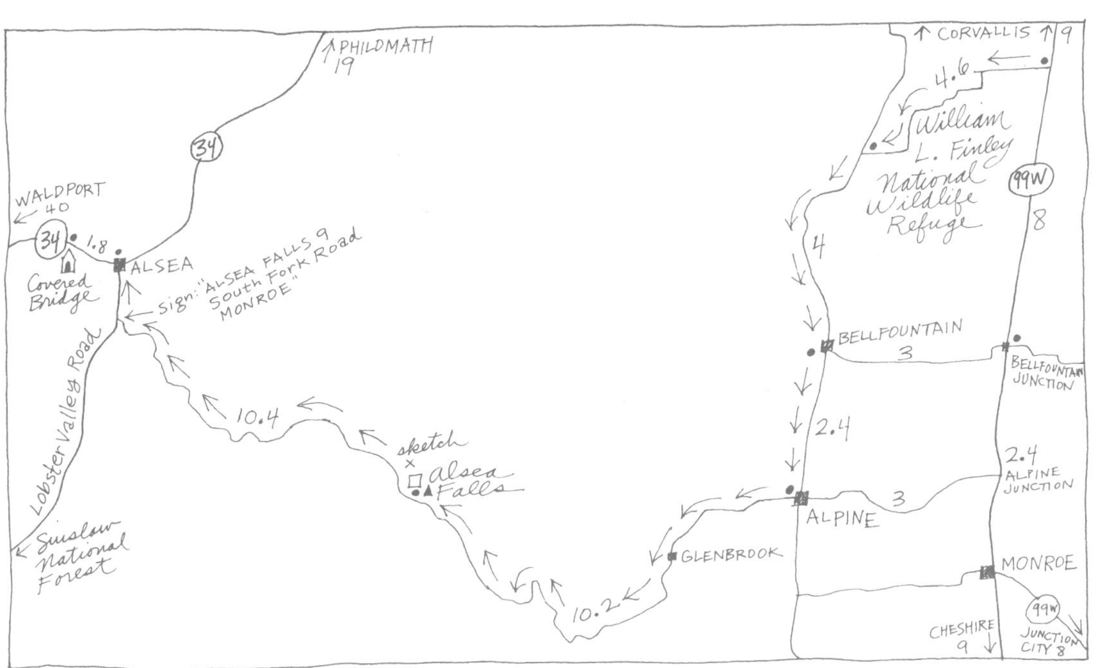
PHILOMATH
19
34
WALDPORT
40
34
1.8
ALSEA
Covered Bridge
Sign: "ALSEA FALLS 9
South Fork Road
MONROE"
Lobster Valley Road
10.4
sketch
×
Alsea Falls
Siuslaw National Forest
10.2
GLENBROOK
CORVALLIS
9
4.6
William L. Finley National Wildlife Refuge
99W
8
4
BELLFOUNTAIN
3
BELLFOUNTAIN JUNCTION
2.4
2.4
ALPINE JUNCTION
ALPINE
3
MONROE
99W
CHESHIRE
9
JUNCTION CITY 8

*Alsea Falls*

The road to
Alsea Falls

South of Corvallis off Highway 99W this back road begins at the William T. Finley National Refuge. This is farming country, then farther on near the falls, forested land. I camped at Alsea Falls and woke next morning to the sounds and sight of a squirrel chewing a green fir cone to bits. While sketching the falls early that day, I saw thousands of caterpillars inching their way over the rocks next to the Alsea River. I had to be careful where I stepped.

Buena Vista Ferry

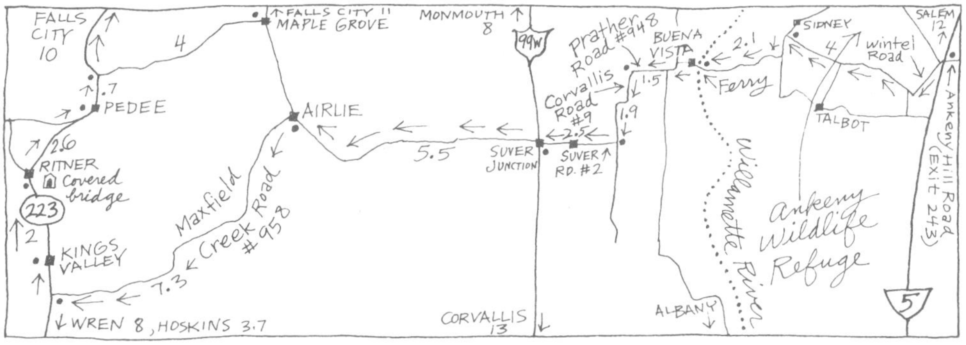

FALLS CITY 10
FALLS CITY 11
MAPLE GROVE
MONMOUTH 8
99W
Prather Road #948
BUENA VISTA
2.1
SIDNEY
4
Wintel Road
SALEM 12
.7
PEDEE
4
AIRLIE
Corvallis Road #9
1.5
Ferry
TALBOT
2.6
RITNER
Covered bridge
5.5
SUVER JUNCTION
2.5
SUVER RD. #2
1.9
Ankeny Hill Road (EXIT 243)
223
2
Maxfield Creek Road #958
Willamette River
Ankeny Wildlife Refuge
KINGS VALLEY
7.3
WREN 8, HOSKINS 3.7
CORVALLIS 13
ALBANY
5

## Road to Kings Valley

Crops of corn, wheat, hops, bush beans, and mint enrich the scenery on the road to Buena Vista.

A cool crossing of the Willamette on the busy ferry begins a pleasant trip to Airlie and Kings Valley.

## To Falls City and Baskett Slough Wildlife Refuge

At the falls a red-haired, freckle-faced boy climbed the waterfall, made a sensational leap clear of the massive rock cliffs to the water below, then scaled the thirty feet of rock cliff to receive my congratulations.

WILLAMINA 14
AMITY 10
turn right on Smithfield Rd. #152
4.6
2.7
.2
Oak Grove Road #7411
22
Baskett Slough Wildlife Refuge
Crowley Road
.7
from Dallas take 223 toward Valley Junction
Bottle Ranch
2.6
POLK STATION
OAK GROVE (see the old church, 1884)
2.1
223
22
99W
ELLENDALE
1.4
22
SALEM 6
Road #20
DALLAS
OAKDALE
4.4
Oakdale Road #20
FALLS CITY
1
Falls City Road #6
Clark Road #868
3.2
FROST ROAD #866
2
223
McTimmond's Road
4
223
AIRLIE 6
.7
PEDEE
KINGS VALLEY 4.6


I sketched the old Hollowell House at 3rd and Pine Streets. Deep blue hyacinths accented the freshly painted white exterior.

Just past the hamlet of Ellendale was Bottle Ranch, adorned with astonishing bottle motifs.

Dallas has an interesting block of historic buildings along its main square.

The old Hollowell House

## The road to Elk City

Elk City is a quiet hamlet along the Yaquina River. You can buy worms at the store and sit on the pier to fish the quiet river. Inspired by Elk City's restfulness, I camped near the store under a great Oregon ash tree where there once had been a sawmill. I awoke in the morning to find a huge local setter pointing directly at me; I guess a stranger in town was not necessarily to be trusted. We made friends, however.

ICE
COLD
ICE
HORSE FEED
FRESH FRUIT
Pork Steaks
WORMS
Regular
76
Unleaded

Elk City store

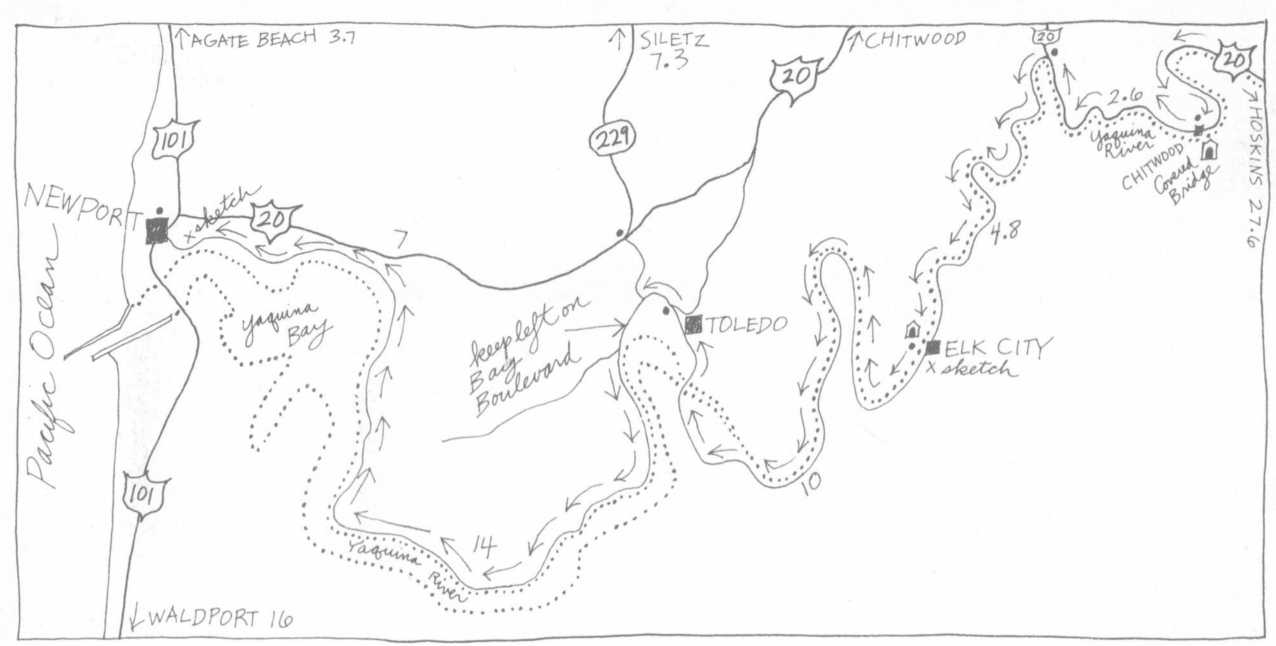
AGATE BEACH 3.7
SILETZ 7.3
CHITWOOD
20
HOSKINS 27.6
101
229
2.6
Yaquina River
CHITWOOD Covered Bridge
NEWPORT
x sketch
7
4.8
Pacific Ocean
Yaquina Bay
keep left on Bay Boulevard
TOLEDO
ELK CITY
x sketch
10
14
Yaquina River
WALDPORT 16

## *Elk City to Newport following the Yaquina*

The road hugged the shore of the river. Mist rose from its surface in the early morning. Hundreds of fishing boats of all kinds were moored or beached near Newport, and fish and shellfish could be purchased at a lively wharf area.

*Yaquina Bay fishing boat*

Wild berry
Scarlet elderberry
Evening primrose

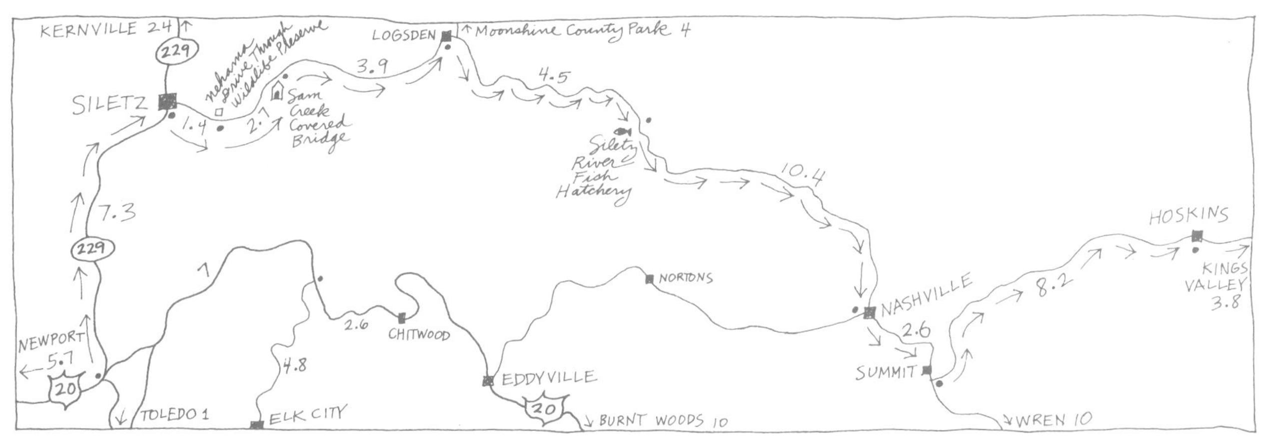
KERNVILLE 24
229
SILETZ
Nehama Drive Through Wildlife Preserve
1.4
2.7
Sam Creek Covered Bridge
3.9
LOGSDEN
Moonshine County Park 4
4.5
Siletz River Fish Hatchery
10.4
7.3
229
NORTONS
HOSKINS
KINGS VALLEY 3.8
8.2
NASHVILLE
2.6
SUMMIT
NEWPORT
5.7
20
2.6
CHITWOOD
4.8
EDDYVILLE
20
TOLEDO 1
ELK CITY
BURNT WOODS 10
WREN 10

*Along the Siletz River to old Fort Hoskins*

On this trip there were meadows and barns and forest, a drive through a wildlife preserve and a silver salmon hatchery. Wildflowers were a continual joy to discover as I sketched.

*Back road ruminants*

## Roundabout to Canby

The Canby Ferry made ten trips as I sat and sketched Mr. Hill piloting the electrically driven M. J. Lee back and forth across the Willamette River. It was a short but pleasant trip, and everyone seemed to enjoy their brief respite from car travel.

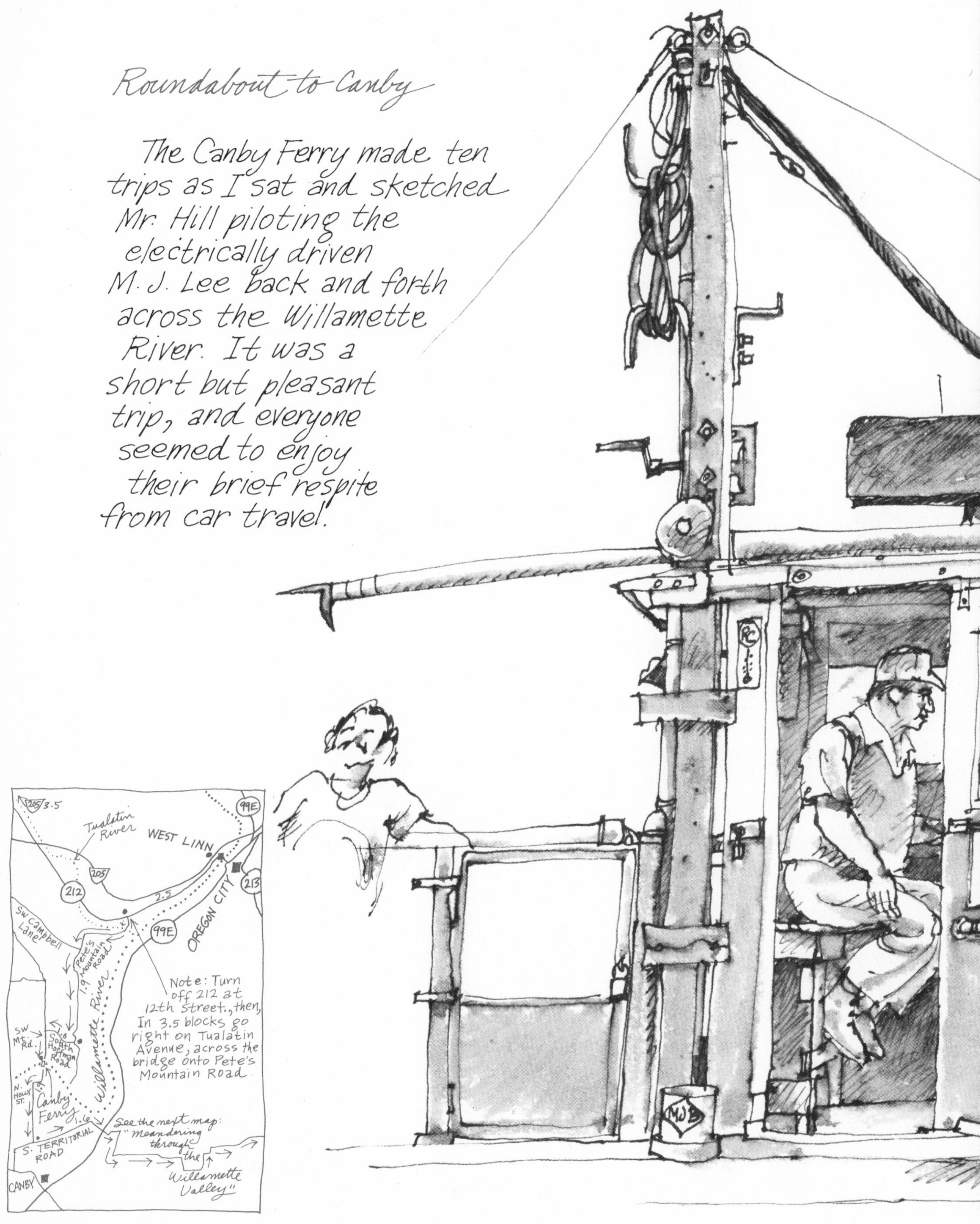

RC
MJB
205 3.5
Tualatin River
WEST LINN
99E
205
212
2.5
213
OREGON CITY
SW Campbell Lane
99E
Pete's Mountain Road
1.9
Willamette River
Note: Turn off 212 at 12th Street., then, In 3.5 blocks go right on Tualatin Avenue, across the bridge onto Pete's Mountain Road
SW Mt. Rd.
1.0
South Hoffman Road
N. HOLLY ST.
1.9
Canby Ferry
1.6
See the next map: "Meandering through the Willamette Valley"
S. TERRITORIAL ROAD
CANBY


Canby Ferry

FREE
LIFE PRESERVERS
IN CABIN
EFC 280
OREGON

Canby Ferry
1.9
1.6
S. Territorial Road
East Territorial Road .6
South Haines Road .6
1.6
South Carus Road 3.4
OREGON CITY 6
CARUS
2.8
South Beaver Creek Road
1.7
FISCHERS MILL
5
Sign: "S LWR HIGHLD RD."
HIGHLAND
S. Lewellen Rd.
.6
1.8
South Bremer Road (views of Mt. Hood)
South Central Point Road .2
BARLOW
99E
AURORA 2
LONE ELDER
MULINO
213
Note: In all practicality I could not include all of the many roads in this area of the Willamette Valley. Please refer to a Marion County map for complete details. This is an accurate account of my trip, however.
CLARKES FOUR CORNERS
South Meyers Road
S. Lewellen Road
1.9
sketch of Kloer barn
South Unger Road
1.2
South Beaver Creek Road
Windy City Road
3.8
UNION MILLS
2
211
ESTACADA
3.5
Rock Creek Church
Smyrna Church
Gordon Road
2.7
S. Dryland Road
1.8 Sconce Road
HAMRICKS CORNER
1.5
211
2.1
MOLALLA
MEADOWBROOK
COLTON
OLD COLTON
CEDARDALE
YODER
S. Cochran Road
South Barlow Road
2.9
South Schneider Road 1.5
Feyrer County Park
1
Darnell-Gibson Road
213
1.3
.3
KOKEL CORNER
South Eagan Road
South Kropf Rd.
South Thompson Road
1
SCOTTS MILLS
South Lee Road
MARQUAM
To Scotts Mills

*Meandering through the Willamette Valley*

The road went through farm and forest land with a stop to sketch at the Kloer ranch, where sheep grazed among the stumps.

The Kloer ranch

At Yoder the amiable Walters family ran the neatly kept old Yoder store.

Not far from here is the 1857 Rock Creek Church set in a historic cemetery. The church is still in use for special occasions.

FARM G
CENTE
Fresh
Brown
EGGS

YODER STORE
ESTABLISHED 1915
Yoder Store
Groceries
General Merchandise
Hardware
Feed
Dry Goods
Frozen Food Lockers
MILK

*North Falls*

## The road to Silver Creek Falls

There are ten falls to see if you hike on all the trails at Silver Creek Falls State Park. One-hundred-thirty-six-foot North Falls is easy to reach via a short trail. One can actually walk around and under the falls to more fully experience its magnificence.

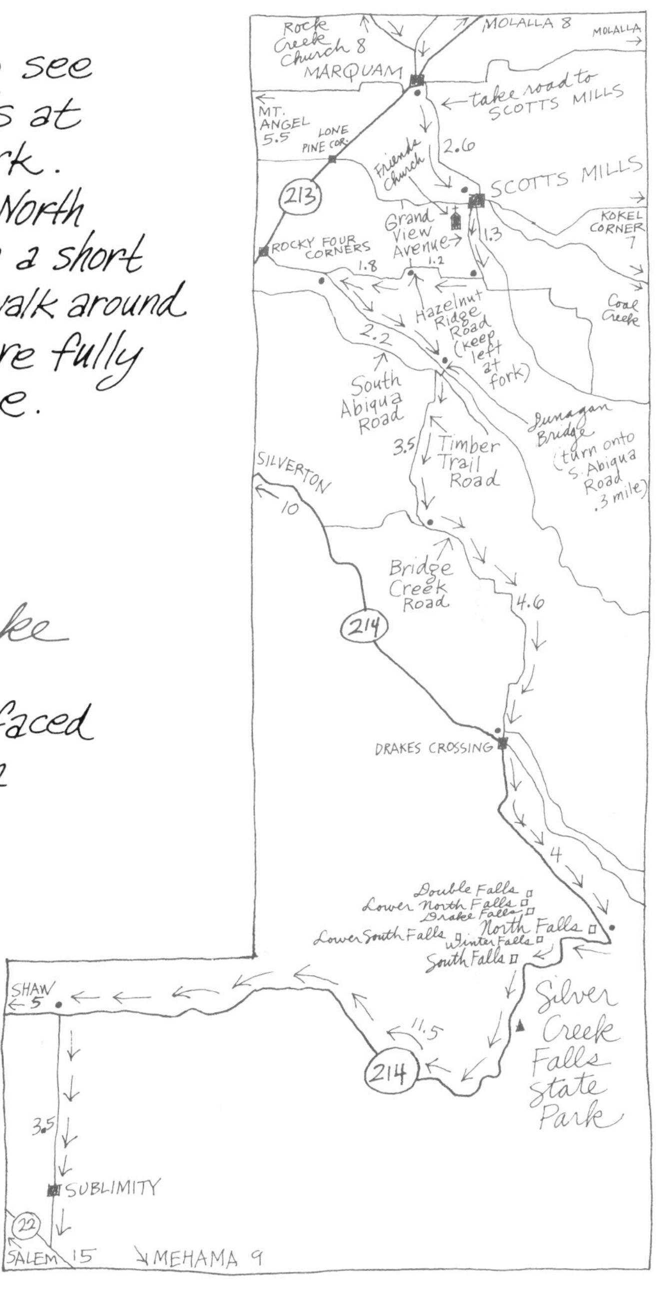

Rock Creek Church 8
MOLALLA 8
MOLALLA
MARQUAM
take road to SCOTTS MILLS
MT. ANGEL 5.5
LONE PINE COR.
2.6
Friends Church
213
SCOTTS MILLS
KOKEL CORNER 7
Grand View Avenue
1.3
ROCKY FOUR CORNERS
1.8
1.2
Coal Creek
Hazelnut Ridge Road (keep left at fork)
2.2
South Abiqua Road
Gunagan Bridge (turn onto S. Abiqua Road .3 mile)
3.5
Timber Trail Road
SILVERTON
10
Bridge Creek Road
4.6
214
DRAKES CROSSING
4
Double Falls
Lower North Falls
Drake Falls
North Falls
Lower South Falls
Winter Falls
South Falls
SHAW 5
Silver Creek Falls State Park
11.5
214
3.5
SUBLIMITY
22
SALEM 15
MEHAMA 9


## The road to Olallie Lake

This was a rough-surfaced road through high mountain scenery to Olallie Lake. The lake was calm. Voices could be heard clearly for long distances across the water. Mt. Jefferson seemed a bit unreal, like a painted backdrop for a stage setting.

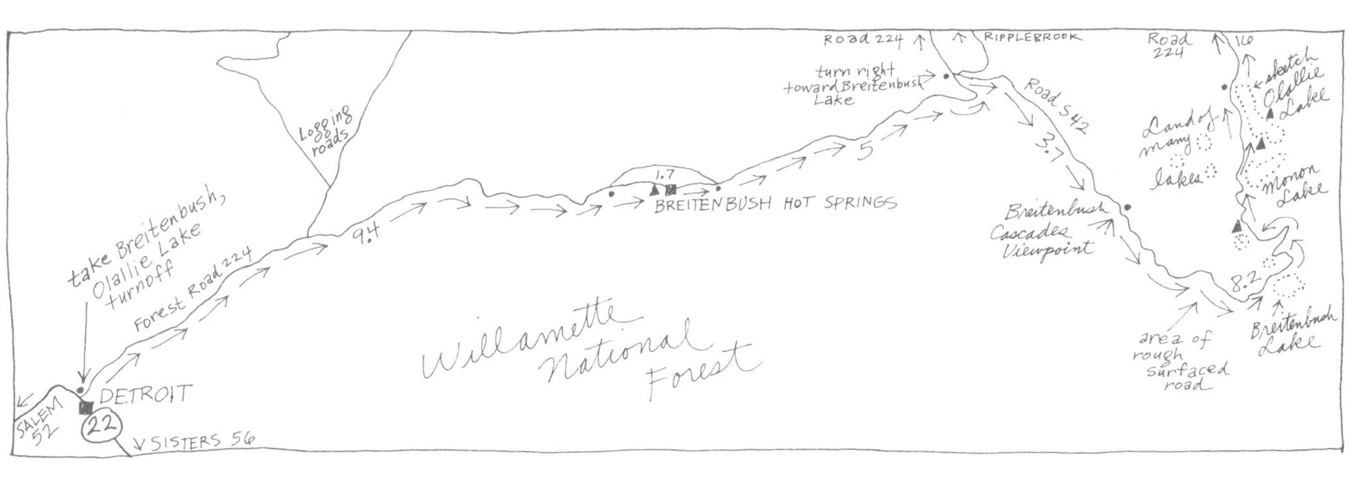

Road 224
RIPPLEBROOK
Road 224
16
turn right toward Breitenbush Lake
Logging roads
Road S42
Olallie Lake
Land of many lakes
3.7
5
1.7
BREITENBUSH HOT SPRINGS
Monon Lake
9.4
Breitenbush Cascades Viewpoint
take Breitenbush, Olallie Lake turnoff
Forest Road 224
8.2
Breitenbush Lake
area of rough surfaced road
Willamette National Forest
DETROIT
SALEM 52
22
SISTERS 56

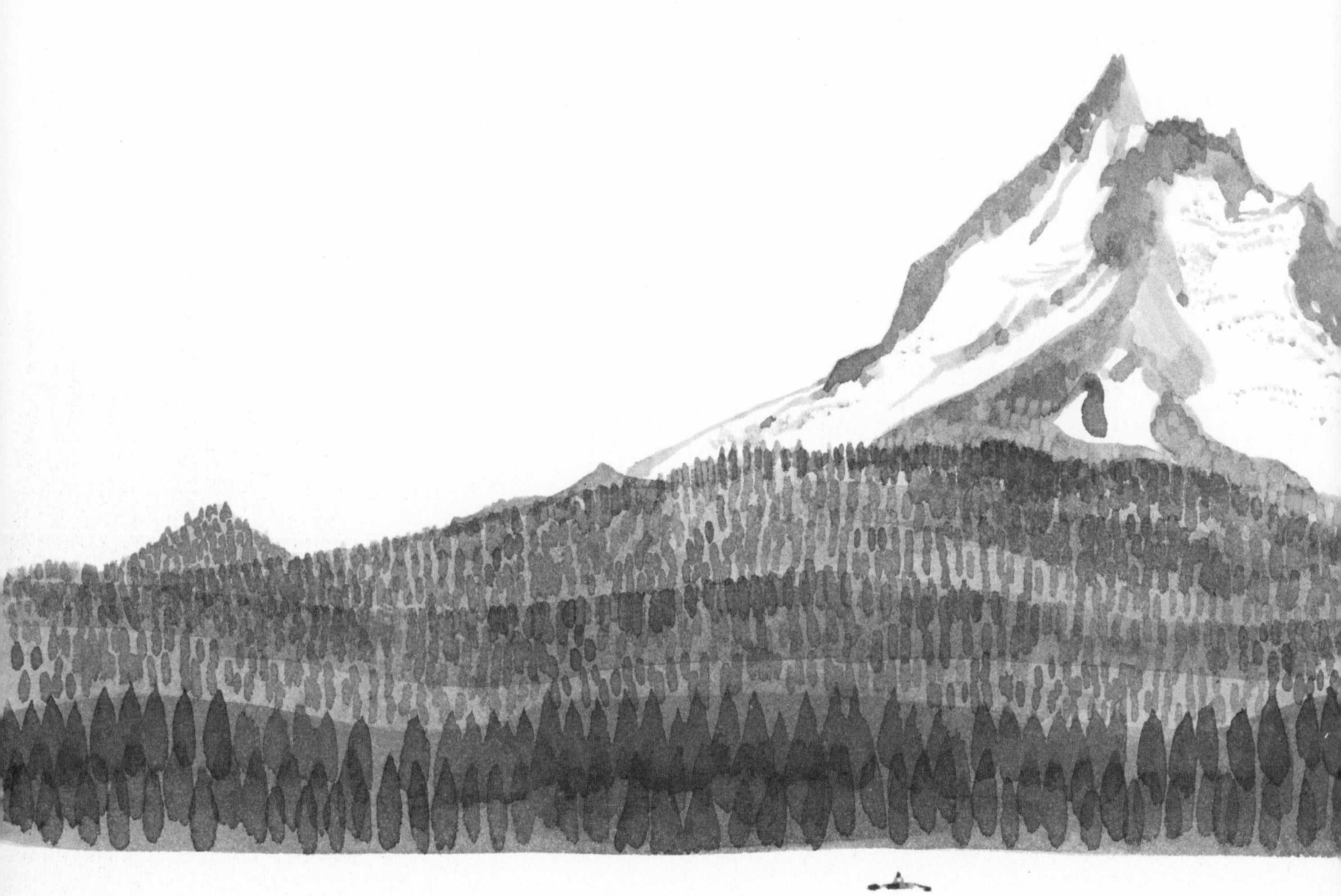

*Olallie Lake and Mount Jefferson*

## a hot springs trip

There were hot springs at Breitenbush, at Austin, and at Bagby. A one-and-one-half-mile trail took me to Bagby Hot Springs. Through the courtesy of Mt. Hood National Forestry Service, there were five separate rooms available for the natural hot baths. Steaming water welled up from the bowels of the earth and flowed past the open window. I pulled the trough bung to fill my big cedar tub, then brought buckets of cold water from the creek to dilute the very hot spring water.

While I soaked in the log tub, thunder rolled and crashed over the Cascades and rain drummed on the roof of the rustic bathhouse -- and I didn't care.

*Bagby Hot Springs*

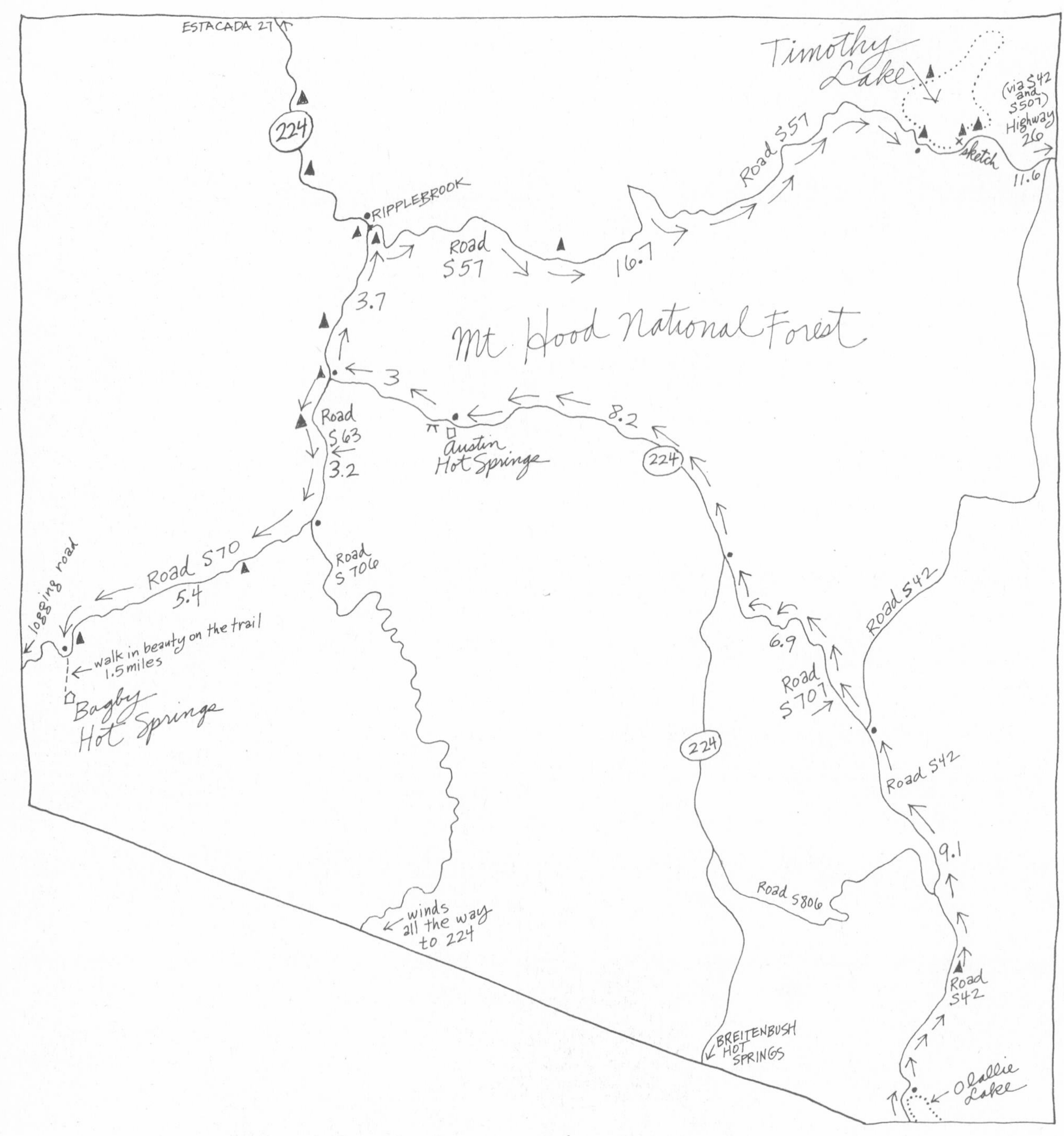

ESTACADA 27
224
Timothy Lake
(via S42 and S507) Highway 26
sketch
11.6
RIPPLEBROOK
Road S57
Road S57
16.7
3.7
Mt. Hood National Forest
3
8.2
Road S63
3.2
Austin Hot Springs
224
Road S70
5.4
Road S706
logging road
walk in beauty on the trail 1.5 miles
Bagby Hot Springs
Road S42
6.9
Road S707
224
Road S42
9.1
Road S806
winds all the way to 224
Road S42
BREITENBUSH HOT SPRINGS
Olallie Lake


## Ripplebrook to Timothy Lake

Mount Hood is a graceful backdrop for Timothy Lake. Motorboats are easily launched on the lake, which is a popular spot for families and fishermen.

## The road to Wapinitia, Wamic, and Tygh Valley

This is great volcanic plateau land, made even more dramatic by occasional gorges that cut across great areas of landscape.

There was thunder and lightning in the distance and threatening rainclouds gathering overhead. It was 7PM, and a farmer I passed was desperately threshing the wheat in his fields to get it in before the deluge.

Earlier I sat on Lloyd and Dixie Woodside's porch in Wapinitia and drew at least one-half of the town, with Mount Hood in the background. Wapinitia was a much larger town in the days when wagoneers hauled freight between The Dalles and Prineville. That traffic ended many years ago, when the new railroad took over the job.

THE DALLES 31
97
Wasco County Fairgrounds
216
12.9
TYGH VALLEY
97
MAUPIN 7
WAMIC
Round barn
cemetery on hill
turn right on Smock Road to Tygh Valley
turn right on White River Road to WAMIC
turn left toward White River and Smock
4.3
3.6
1.2
216
MAUPIN 9
turn left just past store
1.1
216
HWY 26 19
WAPINITIA
12.3
PORTLAND 81
26
6.5
SIMNASHO
Road S400
MADRAS 34
KAH-NEE-TA 13

SHANIKO
HOTEL
SHANIKO HOTEL
LOBBY

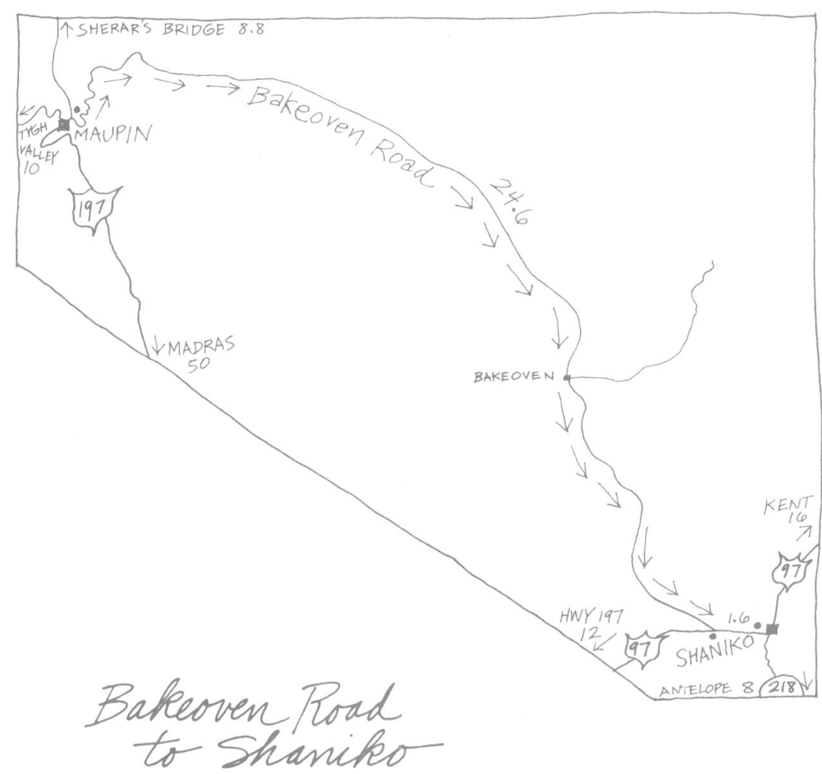
SHERAR'S BRIDGE 8.8
TYGH VALLEY 10
MAUPIN
Bakeoven Road
24.6
197
MADRAS 50
BAKEOVEN
KENT 16
97
1.6
HWY 197 12
97
SHANIKO
ANTELOPE 8
218

Bakeoven Road to Shaniko

I don't think the look of the hotel at Shaniko has changed a great deal since its beginnings. Once called the Columbia Southern Hotel, in 1902 the Shaniko Leader had this to say about it... "This house is a large two-story brick structure, finished throughout with the very best of everything, and is one of the leading hotels in eastern Oregon. On both floors will be found hot and cold water, toilet rooms, bathtubs, etc. It has a fine sewer connection and no refuse or offensive matter can pervade the atmosphere, as is too often noticeable in hotels, especially in the interior."

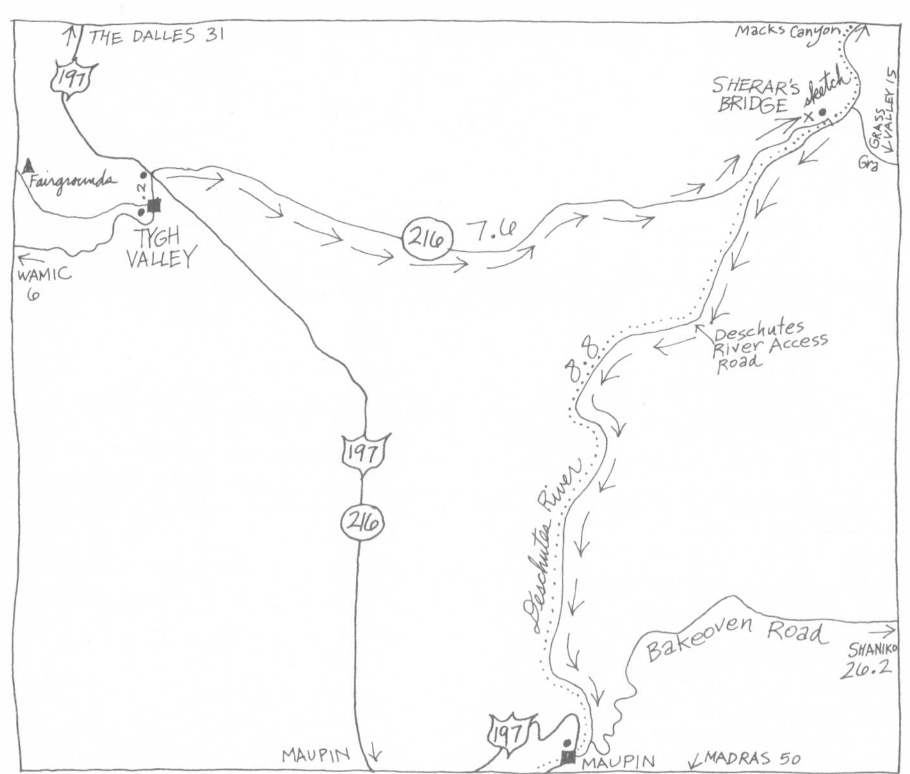
THE DALLES 31
197
Macks Canyon
SHERAR'S BRIDGE
sketch
GRASS VALLEY 15
Gra
Fairgrounds
.2
TYGH VALLEY
216
7.6
WAMIC 6
Deschutes River Access Road
8.8
197
216
Deschutes River
Bakeoven Road
SHANIKO 26.2
197
MAUPIN
MAUPIN
MADRAS 50

*Indians salmon fishing on the Deschutes River*

## Tygh Valley to Sherar's Bridge and Maupin

Near Sherar's Bridge the ancient Indian trail led to a place where the rushing Deschutes River could be forded. The earliest pioneers floated their wagons across this stretch.

Indians were fishing here the day I sketched. They tended great nets amid the pounding turmoil and spray of the river at its frothiest point.

1897

Antelope Community Church

## Antelope and the road to Ashwood

Antelope seemed a peaceful place. I sketched the well-preserved Antelope Community Church to the musical accompaniment of lawn sprinklers, a crowing rooster, and the rustling of cottonwood tree leaves overhead.

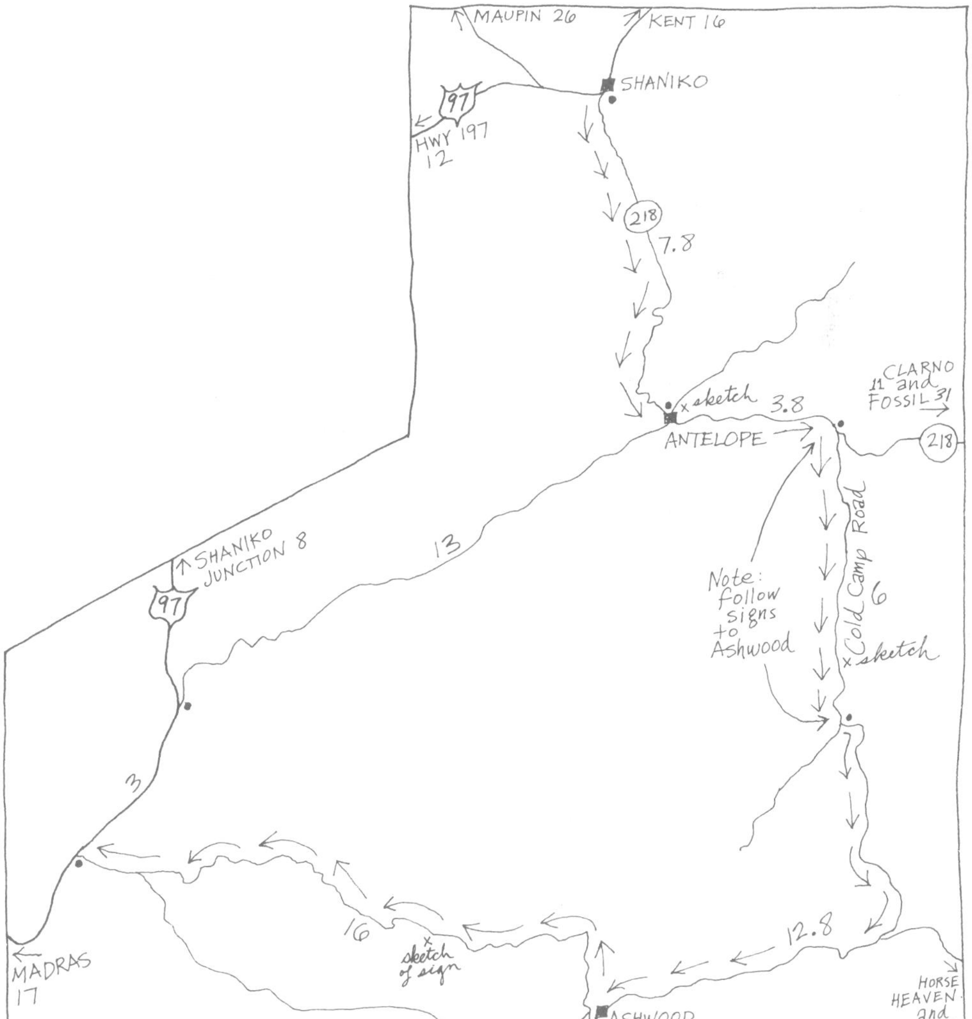

*Road to Ashwood*

The store at Ashwood is half-grocery and half-rock shop, for this is agate and thunderegg country. A thunderegg is a rock that is shaped very roughly like an egg. One must slice it, however, to see the interesting interior pattern.

At her ranch near Ashwood Mrs. Swanson told me that the sign along the road for attracting rock collectors used to read "Eggs and Agate." Since she has changed the sign to "Agate and Eggs" people do not ask for chicken eggs any longer.

SWANSON AGATE & EGGS PRESENTS:
CHIEF PAULINA REDS
VARIETY GOLDS,
BROWNS & BLUES
WITH PLUME, PRETZEL POLKA-DOT + TUBE DESIGN
OPEN

## From Billy Chinook to Wizard Falls and the Head of the Metolius

The air smelled sweet with growing mint around Madras. I sketched the bluffs at Lake Billy Chinook to a chorus of doves in the cliffs in back of me. The road around the lake winds through rock and juniper.

At Wizard Falls you will notice the especially clear quality of the water of the Metolius River. I sketched a yellow monkey flower along the bank while listening to the rushing sound of these purest of waters. The fish hatchery here is one of Oregon's most parklike and was a great pleasure to visit.

Bluffs above Lake Billy Chinook

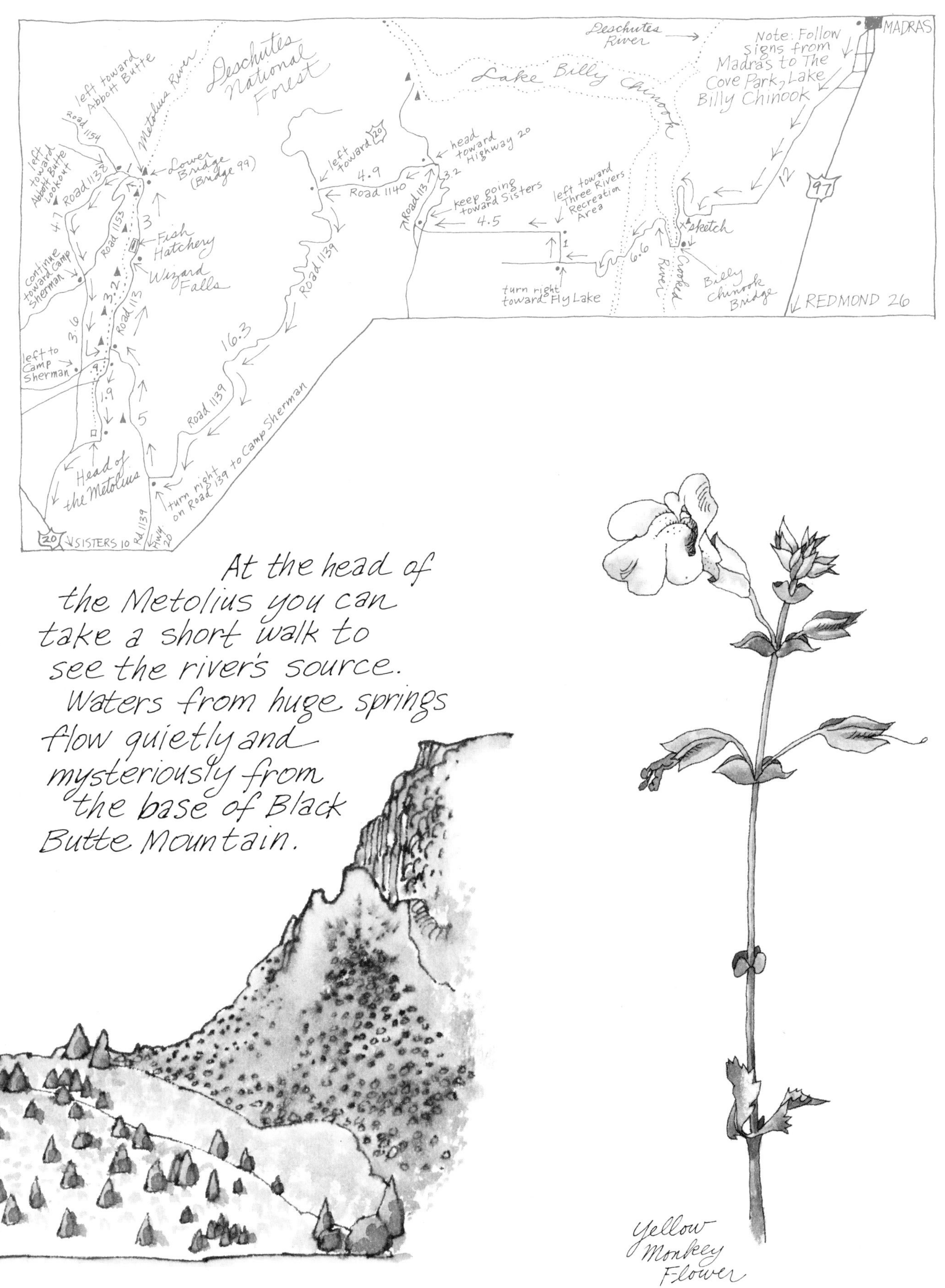
Deschutes River
MADRAS
Note: Follow signs from Madras to The Cove Park, Lake Billy Chinook
Lake Billy Chinook
Deschutes National Forest
Metolius River
left toward Abbott Butte
Road 1154
left toward Abbott Butte Lookout
Road 1138
Lower Bridge (Bridge 99)
1
3
4.7
Road 1153
Fish Hatchery
Wizard Falls
continue toward Camp Sherman
3.2
Road 113
3.6
left to Camp Sherman
.9
1.9
5
Head of the Metolius
turn right on Road 139 to Camp Sherman
Road 1139
Hwy 20
Rd. 1139
20
SISTERS 10
16.3
left toward 20
4.9
Road 1140
head toward Highway 20
3.2
Road 113
keep going toward Sisters
4.5
left toward Three Rivers Recreation Area
1
turn right toward Fly Lake
6.6
Crooked River
sketch
Billy Chinook Bridge
12
97
REDMOND 26
Yellow Monkey Flower

At the head of the Metolius you can take a short walk to see the river's source. Waters from huge springs flow quietly and mysteriously from the base of Black Butte Mountain.

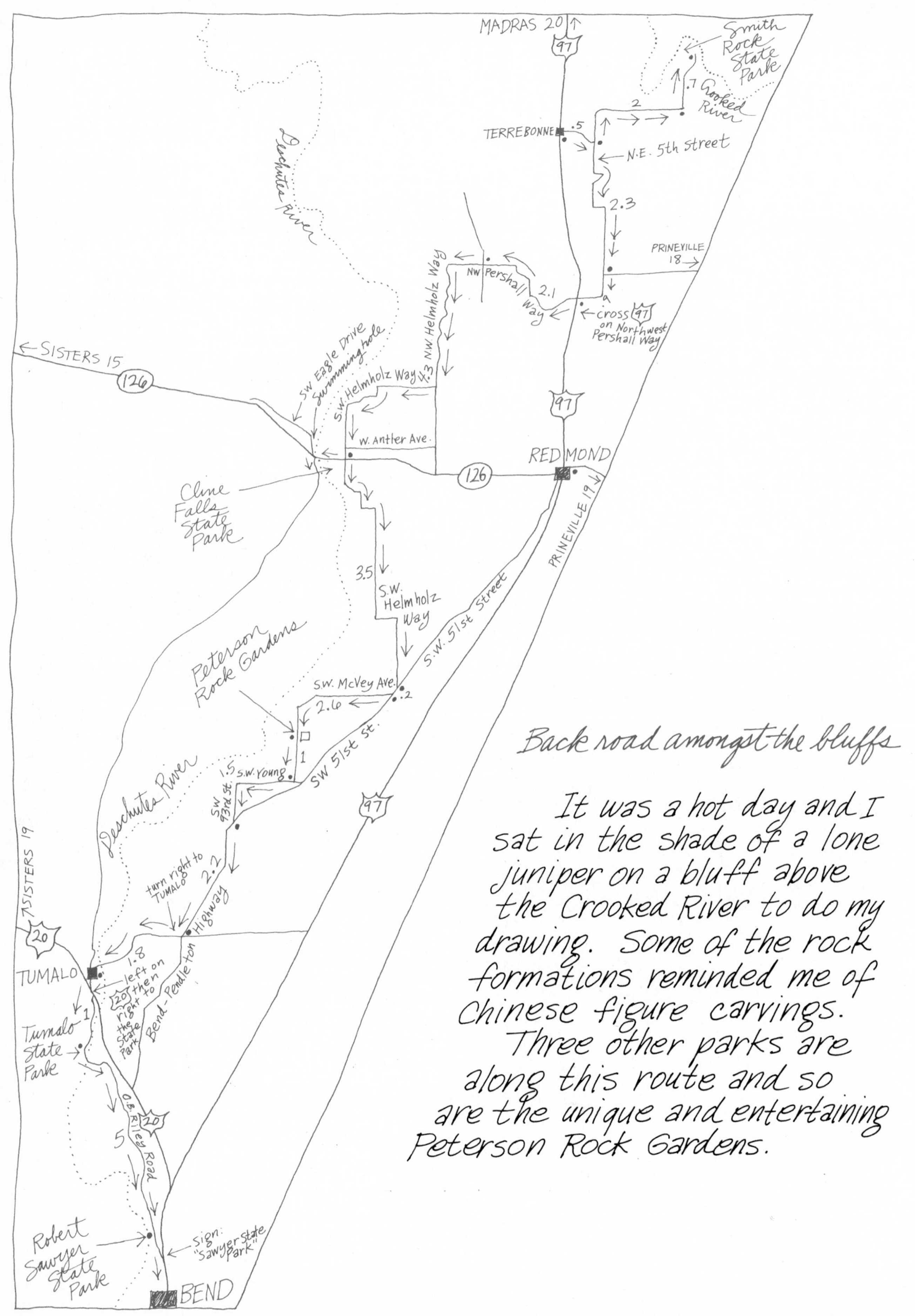

MADRAS 20
97
Smith Rock State Park
Crooked River
TERREBONNE
N.E. 5th Street
Deschutes River
PRINEVILLE 18
NW Pershall Way
NW Helmholz Way
cross 97 on Northwest Pershall Way
SISTERS 15
126
SW Eagle Drive
Swimminghole
S.W. Helmholz Way
W. Antler Ave.
97
REDMOND
126
Cline Falls State Park
PRINEVILLE 19
S.W. Helmholz Way
S.W. 51st Street
Peterson Rock Gardens
SW. McVey Ave.
S.W. Young
SW 51st St.
SW 93rd St.
Deschutes River
SISTERS 19
turn right to TUMALO
Highway
20
TUMALO
left on 20 then right to the State Park
Bend-Pendleton
Tumalo State Park
O.B. Riley Road
20
Robert Sawyer State Park
Sign: "Sawyer State Park"
BEND


## *Back road amongst the bluffs*

It was a hot day and I sat in the shade of a lone juniper on a bluff above the Crooked River to do my drawing. Some of the rock formations reminded me of Chinese figure carvings. Three other parks are along this route and so are the unique and entertaining Peterson Rock Gardens.

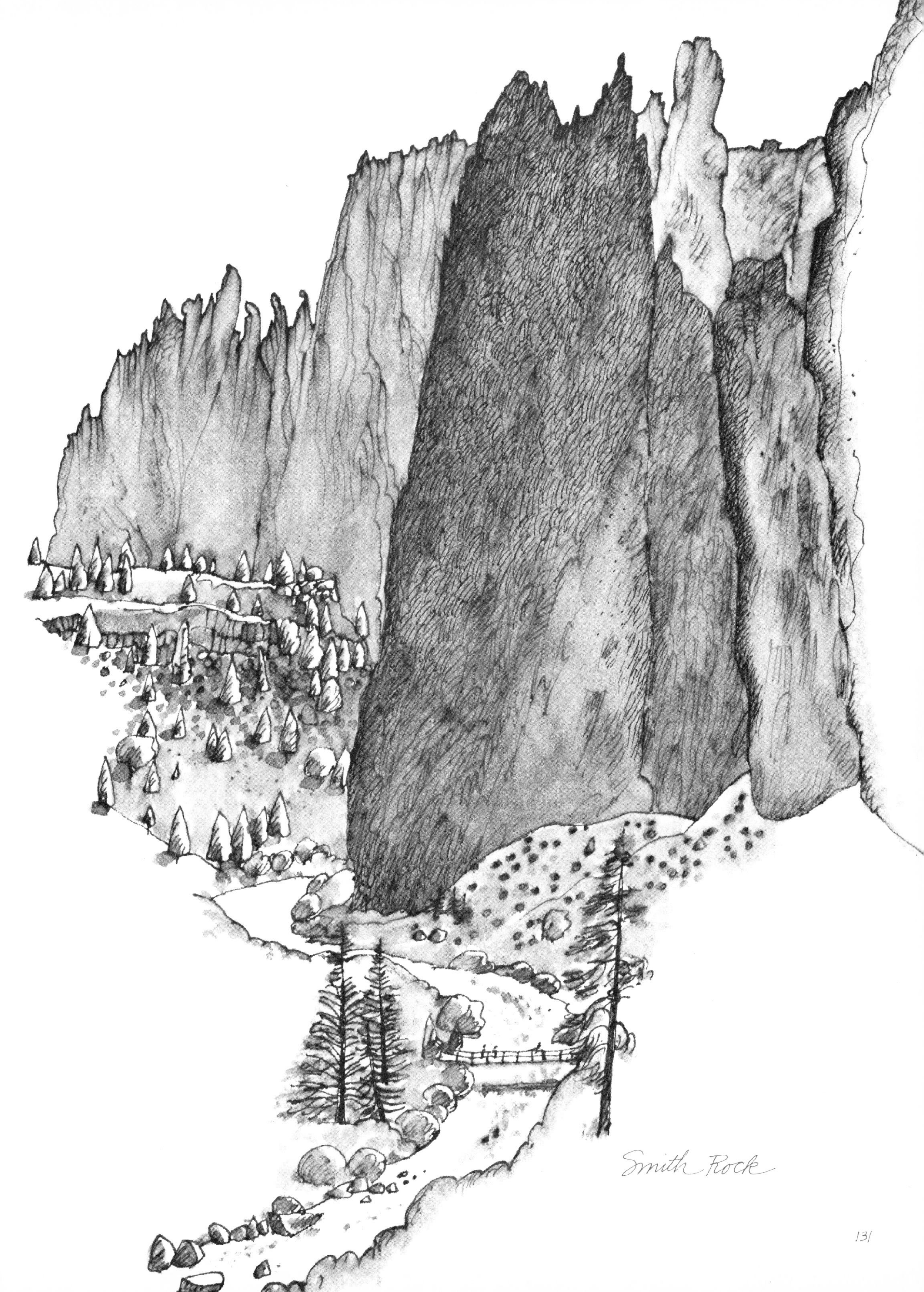
Smith Rock

Stein's Pillar

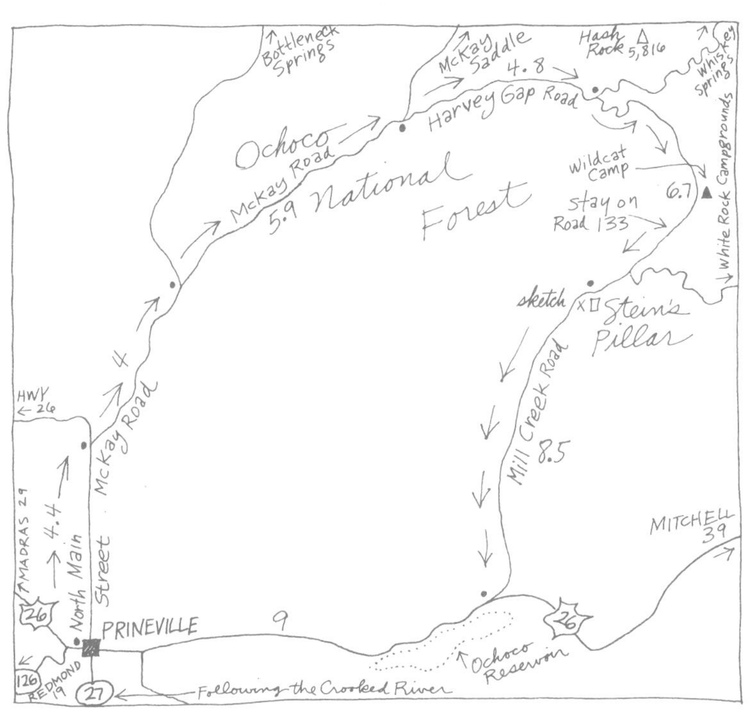

Bottleneck Springs
McKay Saddle
4.8
Hash Rock 5,816
Whiskey Springs
Harvey Gap Road
Ochoco
McKay Road
5.9 National
Forest
Wildcat Camp
6.7
White Rock Campgrounds
stay on Road 133
sketch
Stein's Pillar
Mill Creek Road
8.5
4
McKay Road
HWY 26
MADRAS 29
4.4
North Main Street
26
PRINEVILLE
9
MITCHELL 39
26
Ochoco Reservoir
126
REDMOND 19
27
Following the Crooked River


*The road past Stein's Pillar*

The valley drive past farms and crops soon became forest. On the return journey there was a clear view of Stein's Pillar, a geological oddity towering 350 feet above the floor of the forest.

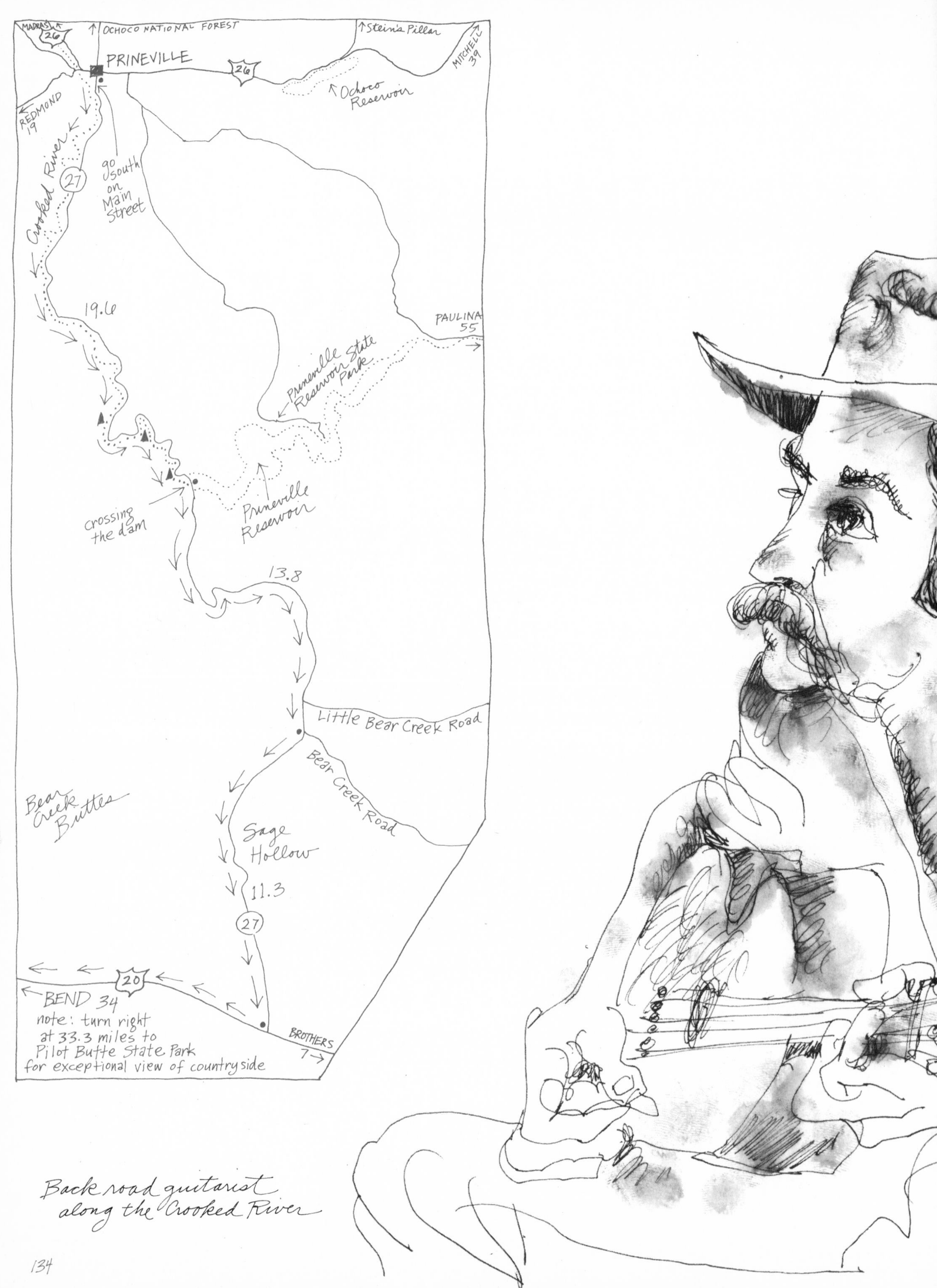
MADRAS
26
OCHOCO NATIONAL FOREST
Stein's Pillar
MITCHELL
39
PRINEVILLE
26
Ochoco Reservoir
REDMOND
19
go south on Main Street
Crooked River
27
19.6
PAULINA
55
Prineville State Reservoir Park
crossing the dam
Prineville Reservoir
13.8
Little Bear Creek Road
Bear Creek Road
Bear Creek Buttes
Sage Hollow
11.3
27
20
BEND 34
note: turn right at 33.3 miles to Pilot Butte State Park for exceptional view of countryside
BROTHERS
7

Back road guitarist along the Crooked River

## Following the Crooked River

Juniper berries were ripening on all the trees in late August. I rubbed the white bloom from a berry to see its rich dark blue color.

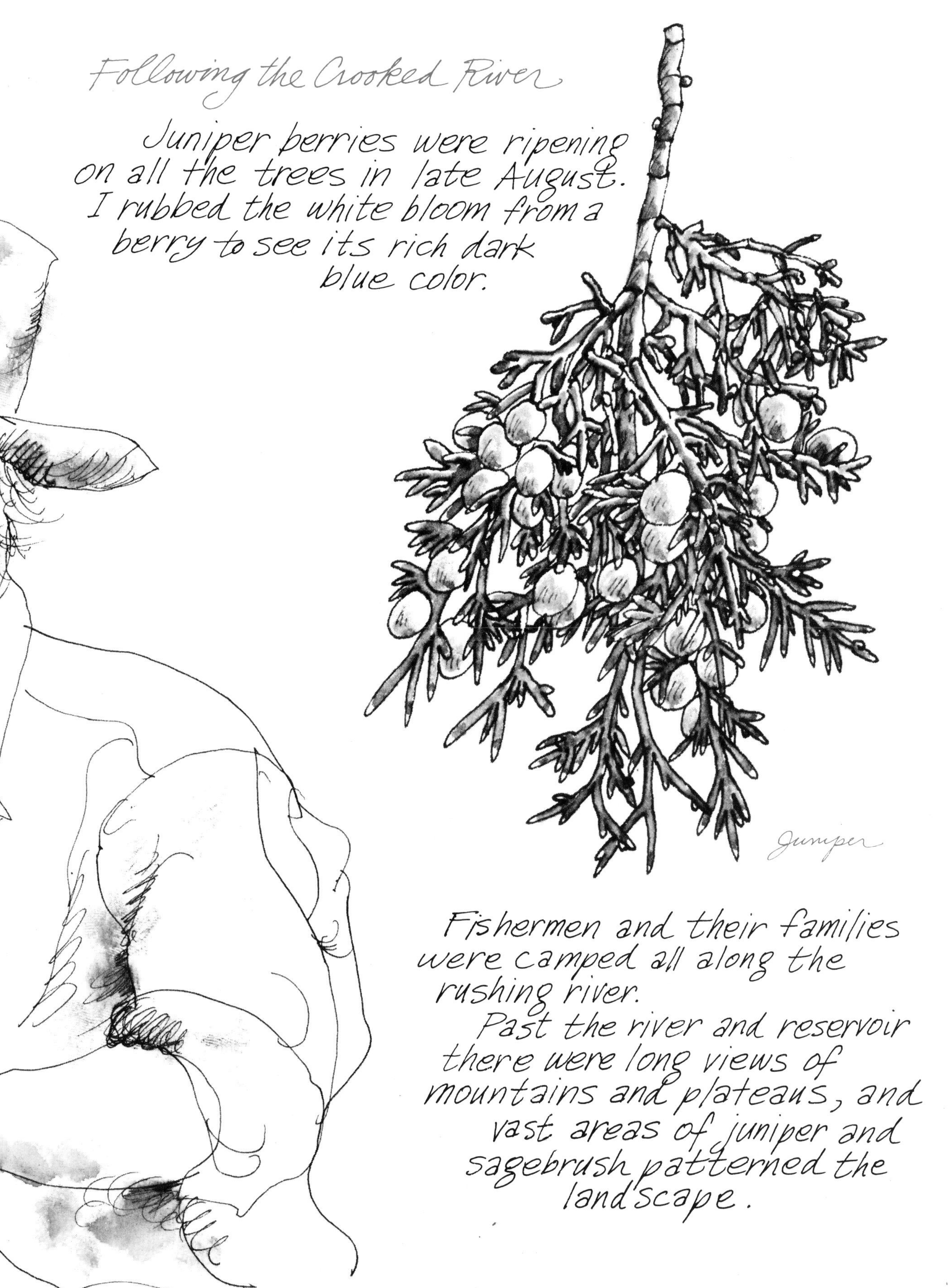
Juniper

Fishermen and their families were camped all along the rushing river.

Past the river and reservoir there were long views of mountains and plateaus, and vast areas of juniper and sagebrush patterned the landscape.

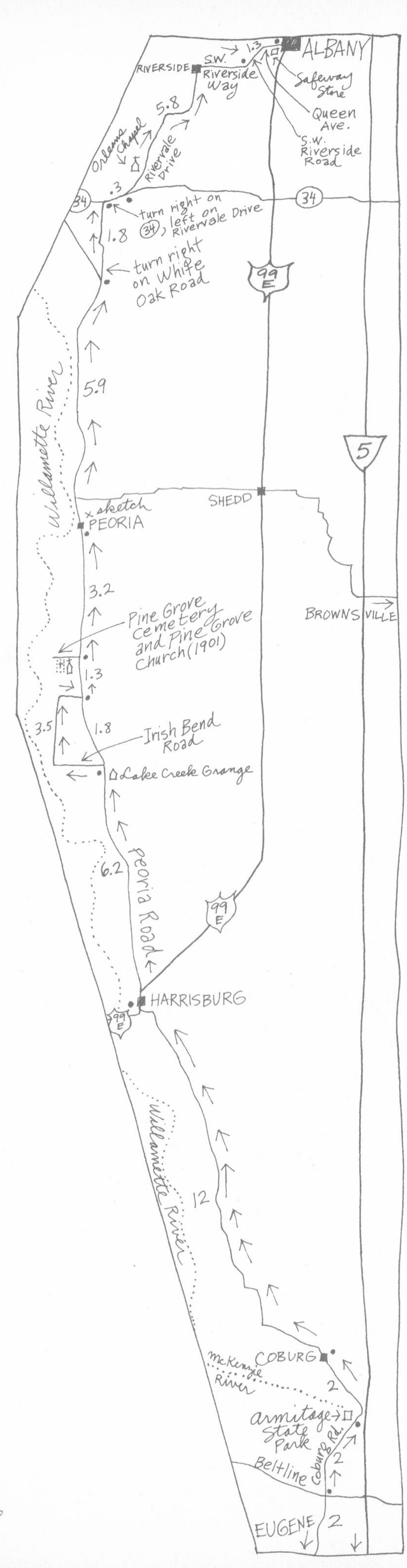

ALBANY
RIVERSIDE
S.W. Riverside Way
1.3
Safeway Store
Queen Ave.
S.W. Riverside Road
5.8
Orleans Chapel
Riverdale Drive
.3
34
turn right on (34), left on Riverdale Drive
1.8
turn right on White Oak Road
99E
5.9
Willamette River
5
x sketch
PEORIA
SHEDD
3.2
BROWNSVILLE
Pine Grove Cemetery and Pine Grove Church (1901)
1.3
3.5
1.8
Irish Bend Road
Lake Creek Grange
6.2
Peoria Road
HARRISBURG
12
Willamette River
COBURG
McKenzie River
2
armitage State Park
Coburg Rd.
Beltline
EUGENE
2


## *Peoria Road and beyond*

This road followed the east bank of the Willamette River past well-kept farms and sweet-smelling fields of mint and clover. I sketched at the drowsy hamlet of Peoria where the General Store sells worms.

OPEN
WORMS


*Peoria General Store*

PEORIA GENERAL STORE

## Roads around and about Brownsville

I sat in the shade of a tree that was heavily decorated with pears to sketch the Blair Hop-curing House. Along with other historic buildings in Brownsville (such as the well-restored Moyer House), it gave me a feeling for times past.

Blair Hop-curing House

This trip meanders along the Calapooia River, offering views of farms and forest landscapes, and opportunities to explore out-of-the-way places. In Brownsville, where residents sit on their front porches of a pleasant evening, there must have been mild speculation as to who was this tourist driving slowly down their street. It would have been better to walk. Then there is more of a chance for a friendly greeting.

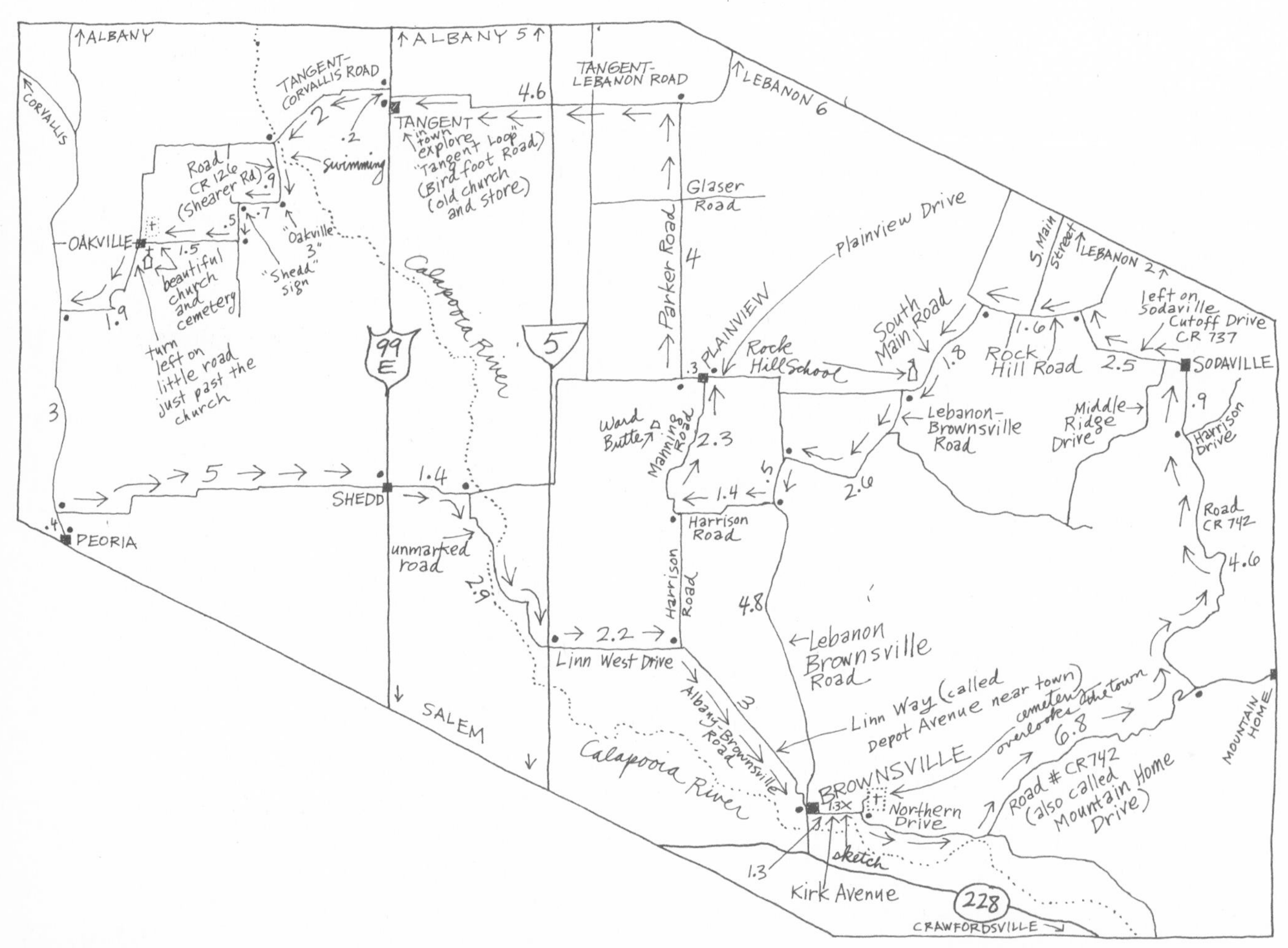

ALBANY
CORVALLIS
ALBANY 5
TANGENT-CORVALLIS ROAD
TANGENT-LEBANON ROAD
LEBANON 6
TANGENT
in town explore "Tangent Loop" (Bird foot Road) (old church and store)
swimming
Road CR 126 (Shearer Rd)
OAKVILLE
beautiful church and cemetery
"Oakville 3"
"Shedd" sign
turn left on little road just past the church
Glaser Road
Parker Road
Plainview Drive
PLAINVIEW
Rock Hill School
South Main Road
S. Main Street
LEBANON 2
left on Sodaville Cutoff Drive CR 737
SODAVILLE
Rock Hill Road
Lebanon-Brownsville Road
Middle Ridge Drive
Harrison Drive
Road CR 742
99 E
5
Calapooia River
Ward Butte
Manning Road
Harrison Road
SHEDD
PEORIA
unmarked road
Linn West Drive
Albany-Brownsville Road
Lebanon Brownsville Road
Linn Way (called Depot Avenue near town)
cemetery overlooks the town
SALEM
Calapooia River
BROWNSVILLE
Northern Drive
Road # CR742 (also called Mountain Home Drive)
MOUNTAIN HOME
sketch
Kirk Avenue
228
CRAWFORDSVILLE

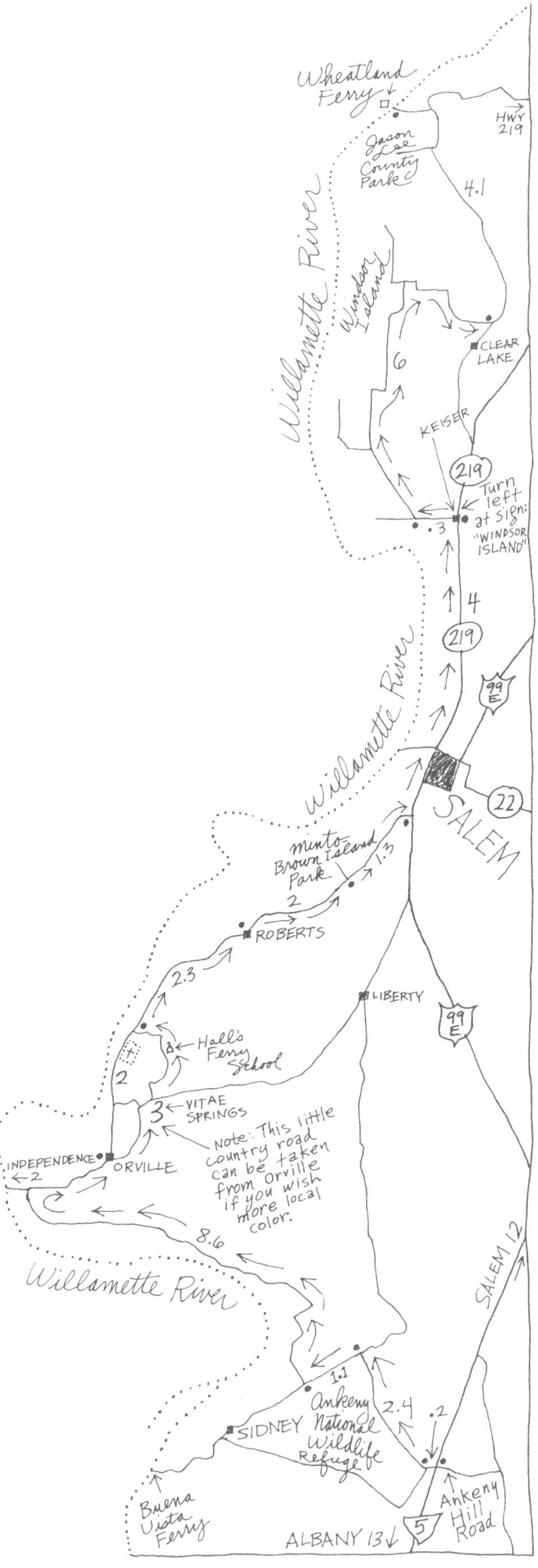

Wheatland Ferry
HWY 219
Jason Lee County Park
4.1
Willamette River
Windsor Island
CLEAR LAKE
6
KEISER
219
Turn left at sign: "WINDSOR ISLAND"
.3
4
219
99 E
Willamette River
Willamette River
SALEM
22
Minto Brown Island Park
1.3
2
ROBERTS
2.3
LIBERTY
Hall's Ferry School
99 E
2
3 ← VITAE SPRINGS
Note: This little country road can be taken from Orville if you wish more local color.
INDEPENDENCE
← 2
ORVILLE
8.6
Willamette River
SALEM 12
1.1
Ankeny National Wildlife Refuge
2.4
.2
SIDNEY
Buena Vista Ferry
ALBANY 13
5
Ankeny Hill Road

Hops

## Rural route to Salem and the Wheatland Ferry

Still following the Willamette north, I was entertained by the view of fertile farm country and the smell of freshly cut crops. Once I stopped to admire fields of decorative, twining hop vines. I sketched some of the green hop cones and leaves. Ripened and dried, these cones impart a pleasant, somewhat bitter flavor to malt liquors.

UNIONVALE
DAYTON 6.6
McMINNVILLE
14
GRAND ISLAND JUNCTION
1.3
2
FOUR CORNERS
x sketch
Grand Island
3.8
221
2.2
PINE TREE CORNER
Willamette River
HOPEWELL
1.1
Maud Williamson State Park
WHEATLAND
Wheatland Ferry
SALEM
12

Smitty's Produce, Grand Island

Grand Island tour

There were so many sprinklers going as I drove along one stretch of this bucolic farm road around Grand Island that I needed to keep my windshield wipers working and windows closed. At Smitty's roadside vegetable stand, Snoopy, the dog, ate a large portion of yellow wax stringbeans as I sketched. Here's hoping Smitty's is still there.

U-PICK
OPEN
U-Pick
BEANS
PICKLES
BEANS
ONIONS
TODAY
OPEN

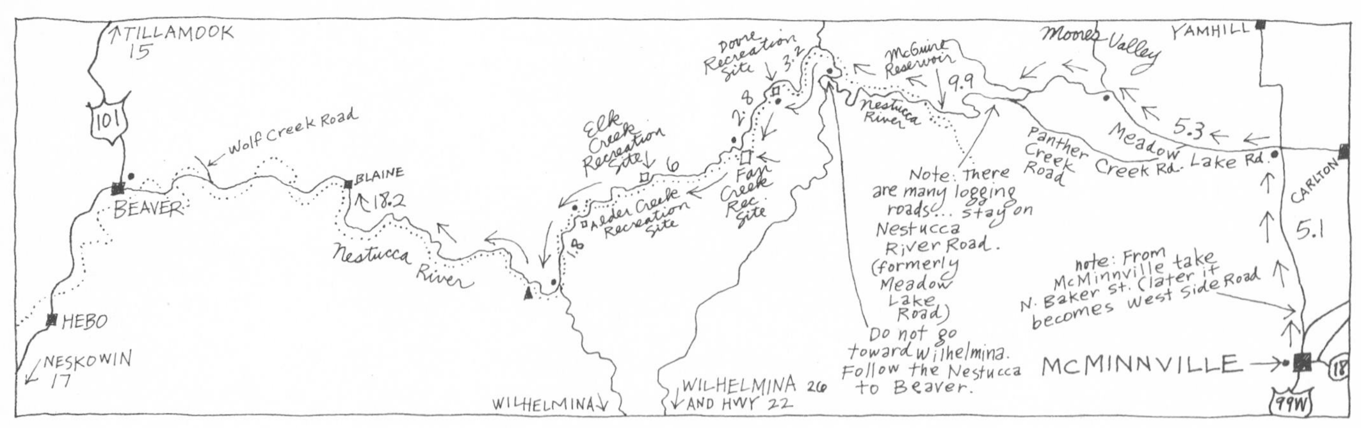
TILLAMOOK 15
101
Wolf Creek Road
BEAVER
BLAINE
18.2
Nestucca River
HEBO
NESKOWIN 17
WILHELMINA
Elk Creek Recreation Site
6
Alder Creek Recreation Site
1.8
Fan Creek Rec Site
2.8
Dovre Recreation Site
3.2
WILHELMINA 26 AND HWY 22
McGuire Reservoir
9.9
Nestucca River
Note: There are many logging roads... stay on Nestucca River Road. (formerly Meadow Lake Road)
Do not go toward Wilhelmina. Follow the Nestucca to Beaver.
Moores Valley
YAMHILL
Panther Creek Road
Meadow Lake Rd.
5.3
CARLTON
5.1
note: From McMinnville take N. Baker St. (later it becomes West Side Road
MCMINNVILLE
18
99W

## *Following the Nestucca River to the coast*

*Leaving the Carlton area there were long views of valleys and farms and big barns. Past the grand panorama of Moore's Valley I headed for the green forests of the Siuslaw National Forest.*

*The road along the Nestucca River led to the town of Beaver.*

*Cows and redwood tree stumps near Beaver*

*Oregon morning glory*

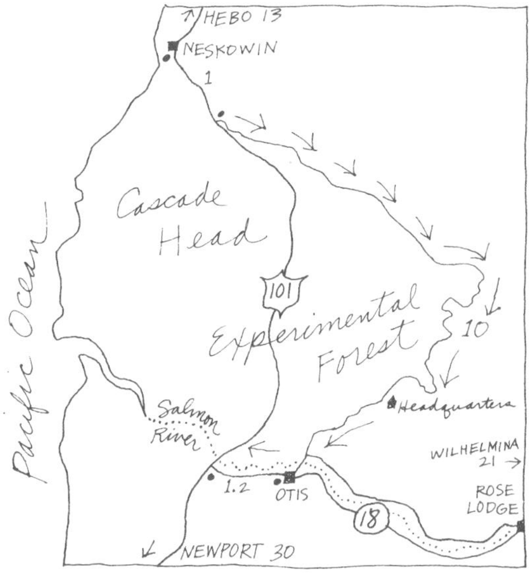

HEBO 13
NESKOWIN
1
Cascade Head
Pacific Ocean
101
Experimental Forest
10
Headquarters
Salmon River
WILHELMINA 21
1.2
OTIS
18
ROSE LODGE
NEWPORT 30

## The scenic drive near Neskowin

This was a trip through Cascade Head Experimental Forest, where research is conducted on the management of Oregon's forest reserves.

I sketched a large morning glory blooming creamy white among berry bushes along the road.

# Three Capes scenic route

At Cape Kiwanda dories on boat trailers awaited their silver-salmon-fishing owners in a storage lot near the beach. Some trailers had rusty old trucks and cars attached to them ready to go, that is, if the aged vehicles could be started. The dories are flat bottomed and are launched from the beach at Kiwanda. The one I selected to sketch was named Dumship.

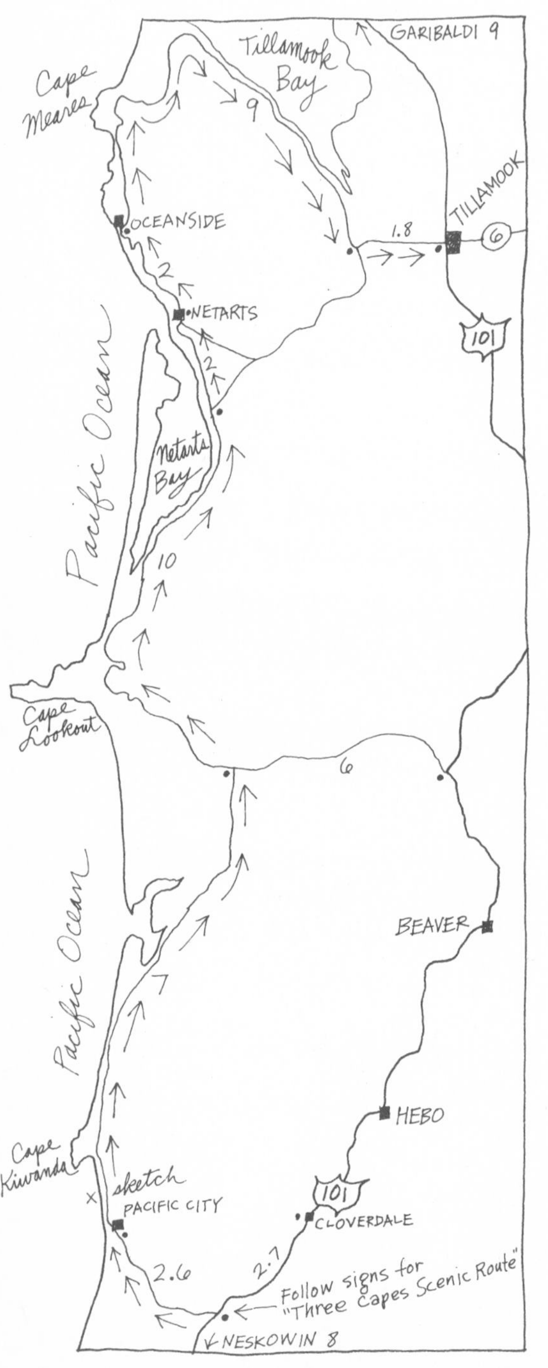
Cape Meares
Tillamook Bay
GARIBALDI 9
9
TILLAMOOK
1.8
6
OCEANSIDE
2
NETARTS
101
2
Pacific Ocean
Netarts Bay
10
Cape Lookout
6
BEAVER
Pacific Ocean
HEBO
Cape Kiwanda
sketch
PACIFIC CITY
101
CLOVERDALE
2.6
2.7
Follow signs for "Three Capes Scenic Route"
NESKOWIN 8

Dumship, Cape Kiwanda

The entire trip was a delight of grand coastal scenery. As I rounded the shores of Tillamook Bay herons were poised in the shallow water, prepared to select any fishy bit that might venture by.

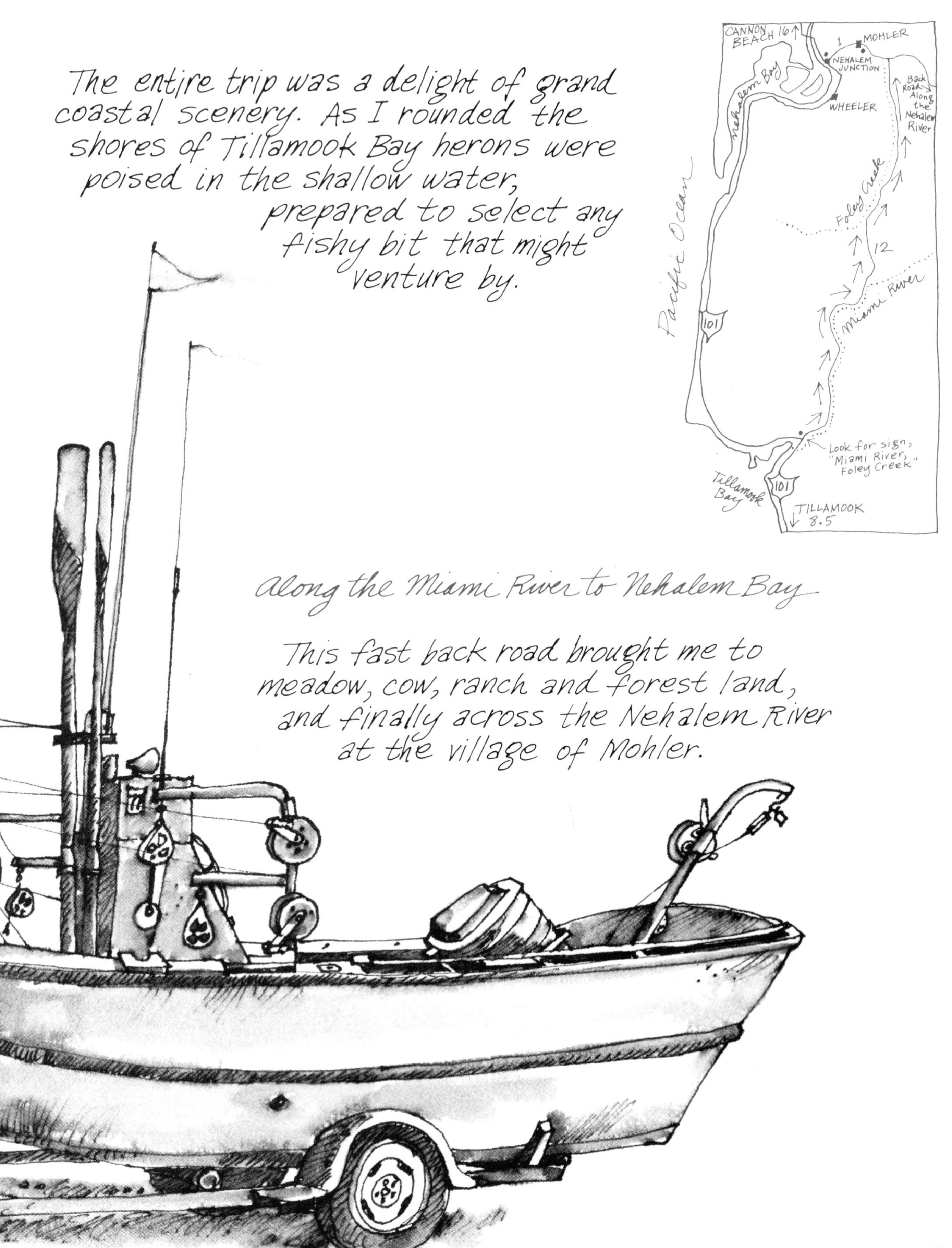
CANNON BEACH 16
1
MOHLER
NEHALEM JUNCTION
Nehalem Bay
WHEELER
Back Road Along the Nehalem River
Pacific Ocean
Foley Creek
12
Miami River
101
Look for sign, "Miami River, Foley Creek"
Tillamook Bay
101
TILLAMOOK 8.5

## Along the Miami River to Nehalem Bay

This fast back road brought me to meadow, cow, ranch and forest land, and finally across the Nehalem River at the village of Mohler.

# Cannon Beach to Ecola State Park

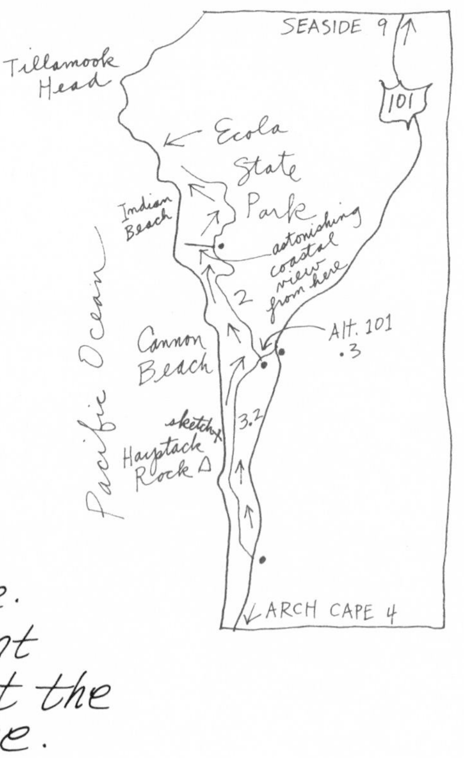
SEASIDE 9
101
Tillamook Head
Ecola State Park
Indian Beach
astonishing coastal view from here
2
Cannon Beach
Alt. 101
.3
sketch
3.2
Haystack Rock
Pacific Ocean
ARCH CAPE 4

I was at work sketching very early in the morning. Birds flocked around Haystack Rock, their cries mingling with the sound of the ocean waves tumbling on the sand. The scene was intriguing to both ear and eye. Later at the overlook point in Ecola Park I marveled at the beauty of the Oregon coastline.

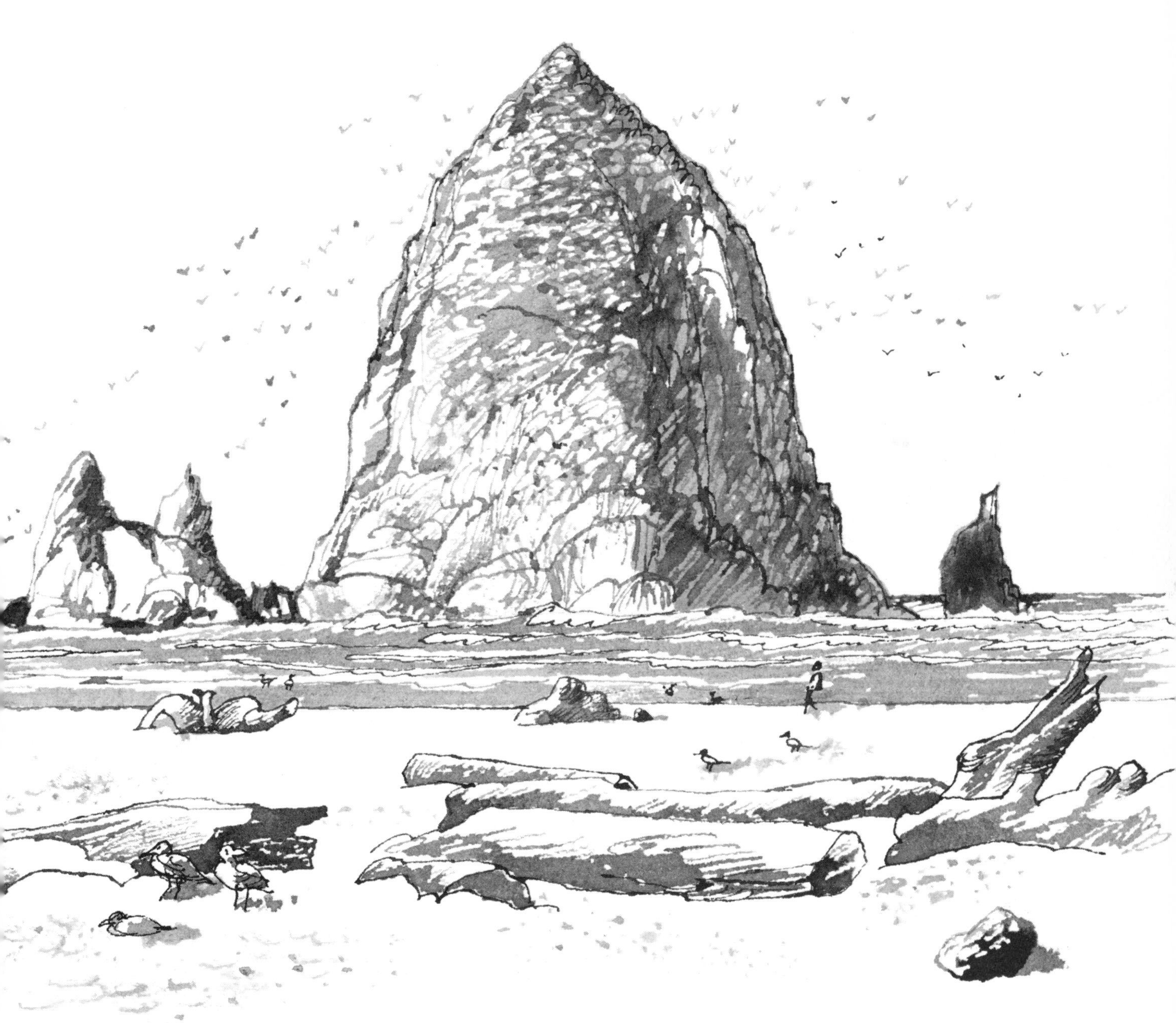

*Haystack Rock*

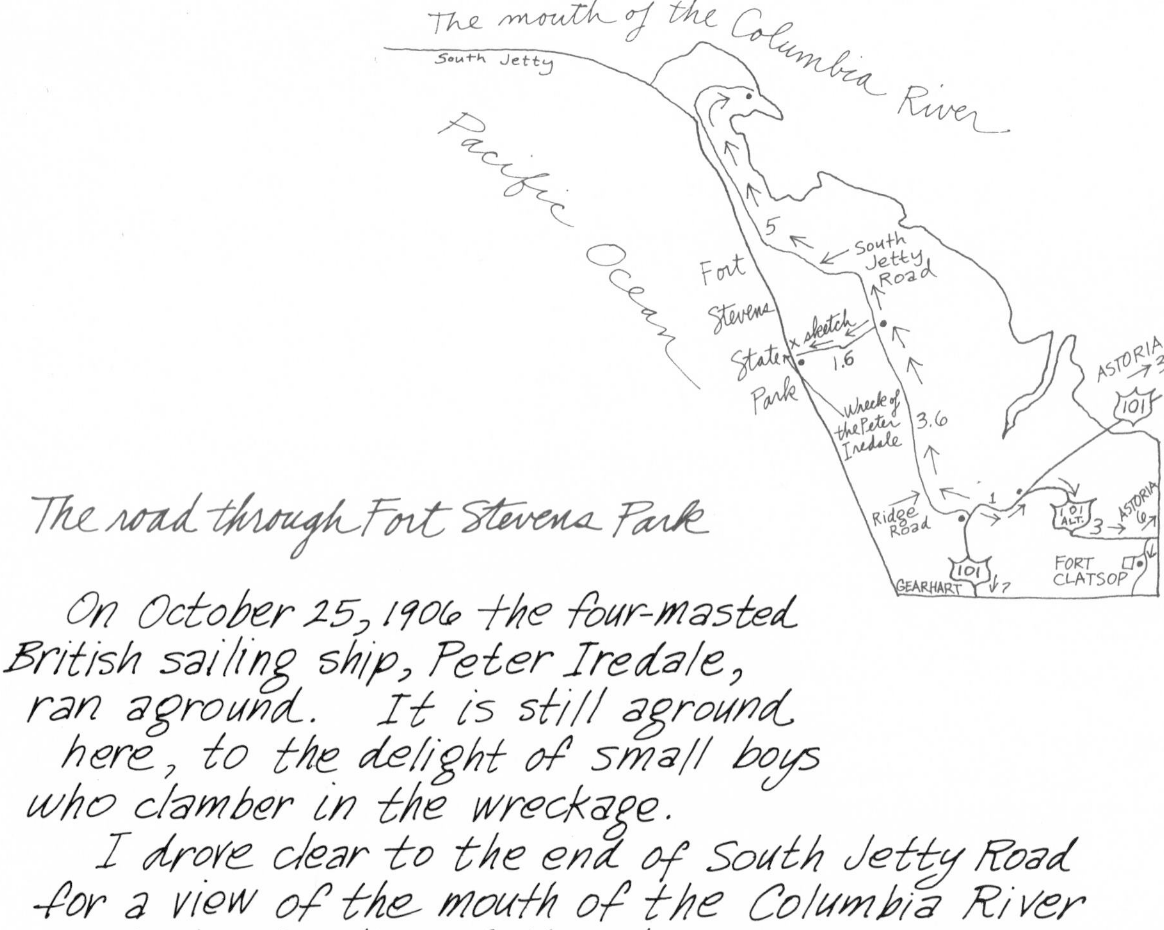
The mouth of the Columbia River
South Jetty
Pacific Ocean
Fort Stevens State Park
South Jetty Road
5
x sketch
1.6
Wreck of the Peter Iredale
3.6
ASTORIA 3
101
Ridge Road
1
101 ALT.
3
ASTORIA 6
FORT CLATSOP
GEARHART
101
7

The road through Fort Stevens Park

On October 25, 1906 the four-masted British sailing ship, Peter Iredale, ran aground. It is still aground here, to the delight of small boys who clamber in the wreckage.

I drove clear to the end of South Jetty Road for a view of the mouth of the Columbia River and the shoreline of the state of Washington.

The re-creation of Lewis and Clark's winter headquarters at Fort Clatsop was the next thing to see.

The wreck of the Peter Iredale

## Young's River Loop and Walluski Loop, too

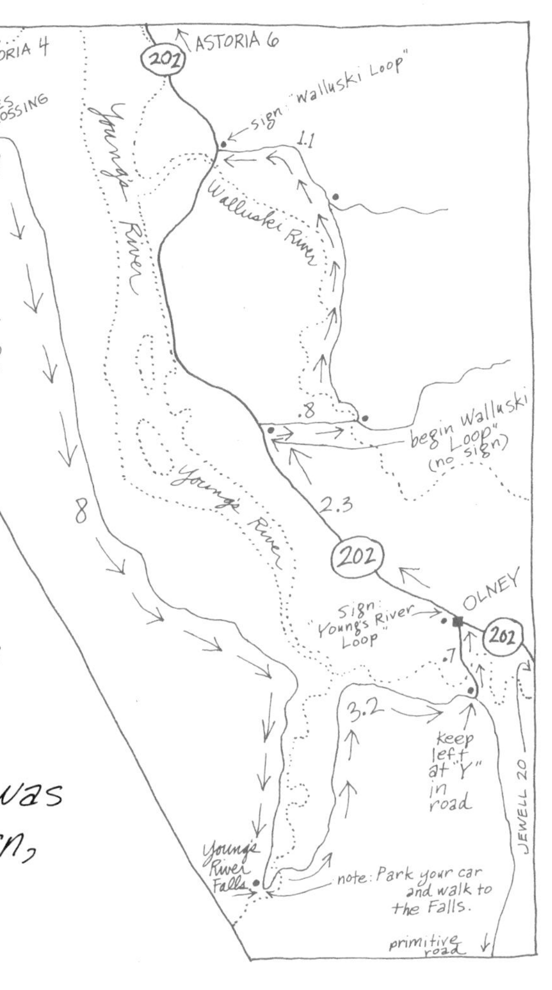

ASTORIA 4
ASTORIA 6
201
101 ALT.
101 ALT
MILES CROSSING
Fort Clatsop 3
SEASIDE 14
sign: "Walluski Loop"
1.1
Walluski River
Young's River
Begin Young's River Loop
8
.8
begin Walluski Loop" (no sign)
2.3
202
OLNEY
Sign: "Young's River Loop"
202
.7
3.2
keep left at "Y" in road
JEWELL 20
Young's River Falls
note: Park your car and walk to the Falls.
primitive road


Along Young's River I made a picture of an old barn, now minus its silo, but still in use and appreciated by both cows and artists alike.

I stopped to view Young's River Falls. A number of cars were parked nearby and I discovered their occupants swimming and splashing at the base of the roaring falls.

The Walluski Loop drive was a visual feast of farm and barn, stream and slough.

*Young's River*

Buttercup

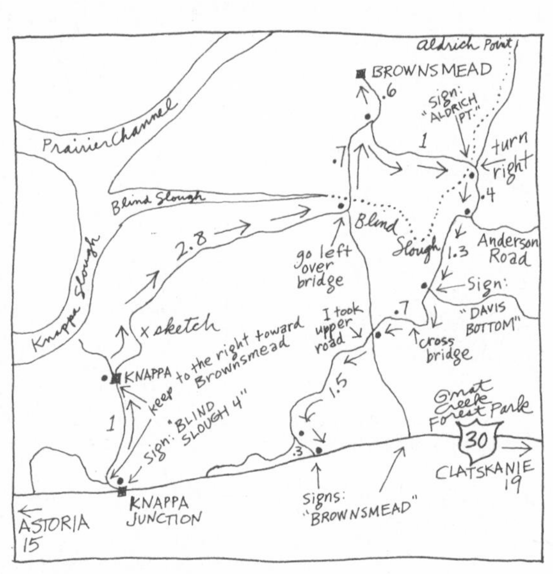
Aldrich Point
BROWNSMEAD
.6
Sign: "ALDRICH PT."
Prairie Channel
1
turn right
.7
Blind Slough
.4
Blind Slough
2.8
go left over bridge
Anderson Road
1.3
Knappa Slough
Sign: "DAVIS BOTTOM"
x sketch
.7
I took upper road
cross bridge
KNAPPA
keep to the right toward Brownsmead
1.5
Sign: "BLIND SLOUGH 4"
1
Gnat Creek Forest Park
30
.3
CLATSKANIE 19
KNAPPA JUNCTION
Signs: "BROWNSMEAD"
ASTORIA 15

Bob Ziak's sign near Brownsmead

## The road to Brownsmead

While I was drawing this scene, Mr. Ziak came by in his tractor. When he realized I was sketching his Canadian goose nest, woodduck house, and sign, he marched, hammer in hand, to nail up the last part of his message, which had fallen down. The complete sign then read, "This land dedicated to the song of birds, the sound of wings to all of nature's creatures, for the joy their presence brings. No hunting. Bob Ziak." It was the gentlest exhortation not to hunt on private property that I had ever seen.

This was a lovely area of waterways and meadows for me to enjoy.

NOTICE
THIS LAND
DEDICATED TO
THE SONG OF BIRDS
THE SOUND OF WINGS
TO ALL OF NATURES
CREATURES FOR THE JOY

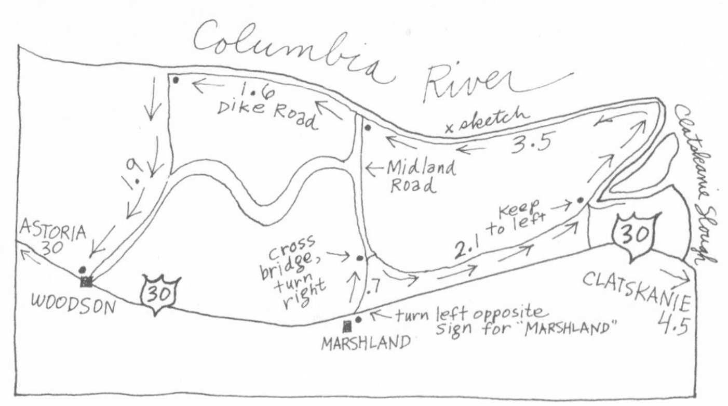
Columbia River
1.6
Dike Road
x sketch
3.5
Clatskanie Slough
Midland Road
1.9
Keep to left
ASTORIA 30
30
cross bridge, turn right
2.1
.7
WOODSON
30
CLATSKANIE 4.5
turn left opposite sign for "MARSHLAND"
MARSHLAND

*Levee back road along the Columbia*

Trees seem to grow out of old pilings in the Columbia River. I saw a great many that day.

The Columbia River retains its majesty even though man has it pretty well under control. At several points I had the feeling I was seeing the great river as it was in Lewis and Clark's day, until an oil tanker would slip around the bend.

The Columbia River

## Side road past Mayger on the Columbia

On Depot Street, just off the road to Mayger, I sketched the Clatskanie Depot. I was hoping a train would come by, but there was no such luck.

At Mayger Downing Church I ate lunch and inspected headstones in the the graveyard.

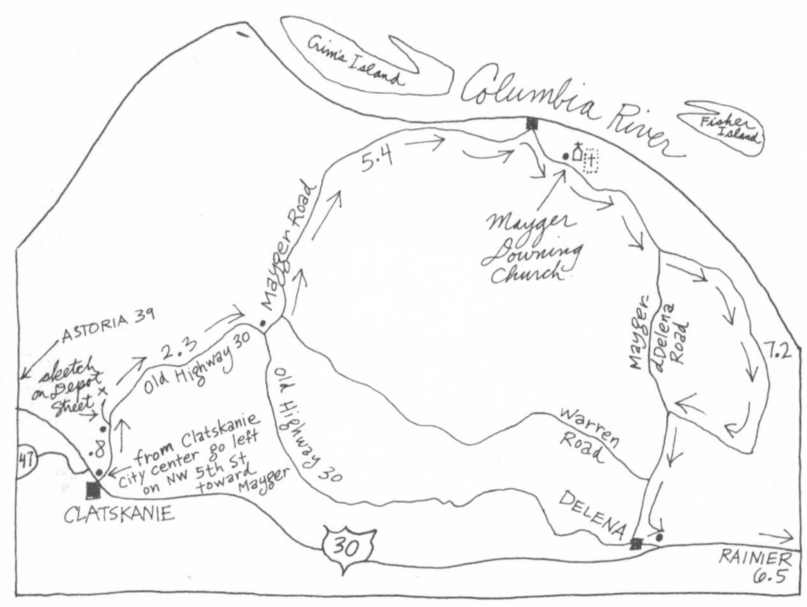
Grim's Island
Columbia River
Fisher Island
5.4
Mayger Road
Mayger Downing Church
ASTORIA 39
2.3
Old Highway 30
sketch on Depot Street
.8
47
from Clatskanie City center go left on NW 5th St toward Mayger
CLATSKANIE
Old Highway 30
Warren Road
Mayger-Delena Road
7.2
DELENA
30
RAINIER 6.5

The old depot

CLATSKANIE

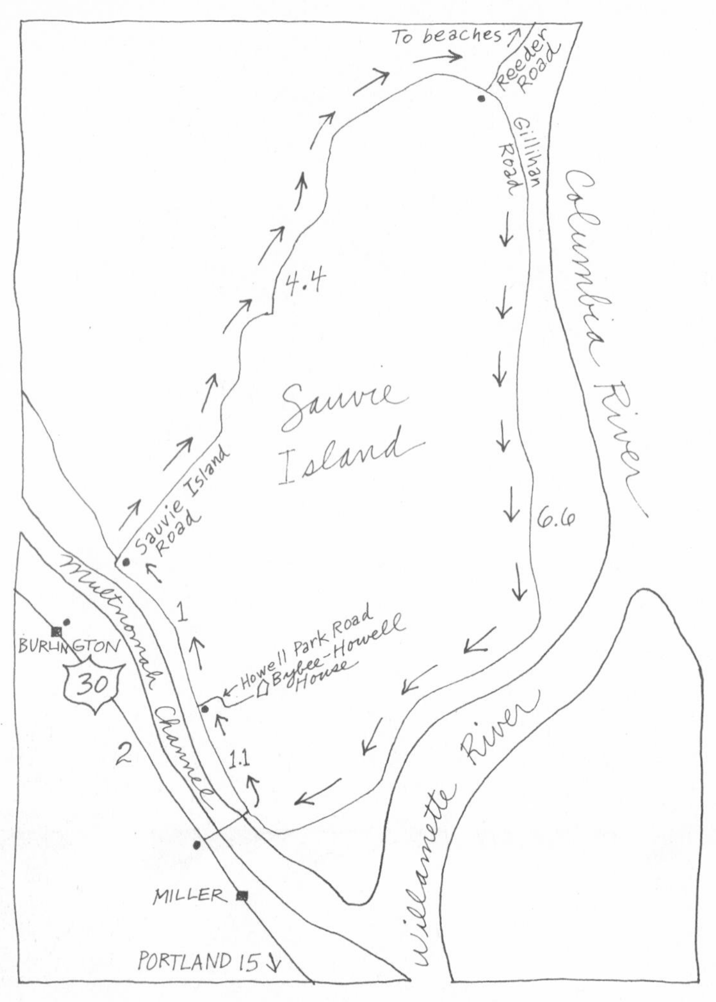
To beaches
Reeder Road
Gillihan Road
Columbia River
4.4
Sauvie Island
Sauvie Island Road
6.6
Multnomah Channel
1
BURLINGTON
30
Howell Park Road
Bybee-Howell House
2
1.1
Willamette River
MILLER
PORTLAND 15

## Sauvie Island journey

I stopped to visit the Bybee-Howell house while traveling around Sauvie Island. It was named after two families that had lived there since it was built in 1856. This historic house is presently maintained by the Oregon Historical Society for Multnomah County and is open to the public. The 1860 doll looking at you in my picture was sitting in a rocking chair in one of the upper rooms.

I passed many vegetable farms and paused at the popular beaches along the Columbia River.

The doll, 1860

ELFORD

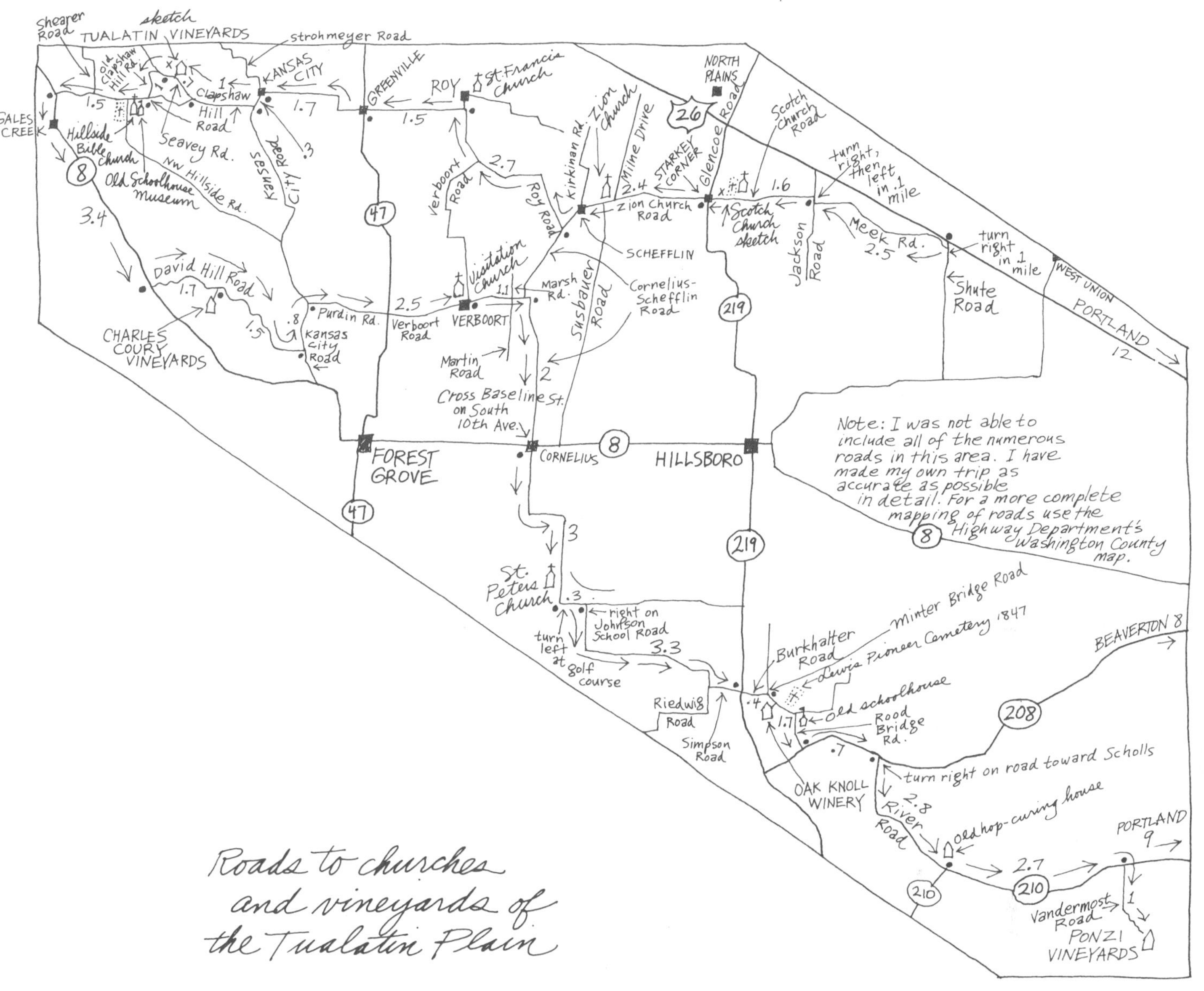

Shearer Road
sketch
TUALATIN VINEYARDS
Strohmeyer Road
KANSAS CITY
Old Clapshaw Hill Rd.
Clapshaw
Hill Road
GALES CREEK
Hillside Bible Church
Seavey Rd.
Old Schoolhouse museum
NW Hillside Rd.
Kansas City Road
GREENVILLE
ROY
St. Francis Church
NORTH PLAINS
26
Kirkinan Rd.
Zion Church
Milne Drive
STARKEY CORNER
Glencoe Road
Scotch Church Road
turn right, then left in .1 mile
Verboort Road
Roy Road
Zion Church Road
Scotch Church sketch
Jackson Road
Meek Rd.
turn right in .1 mile
WEST UNION
47
SCHEFFLIN
Visitation Church
Marsh Rd.
Cornelius-Schefflin Road
Susbauer Road
Shute Road
PORTLAND 12
David Hill Road
Purdin Rd.
Verboort Road
VERBOORT
219
CHARLES COURY VINEYARDS
Kansas City Road
Martin Road
Cross Baseline St. on South 10th Ave.
FOREST GROVE
CORNELIUS
8
HILLSBORO
Note: I was not able to include all of the numerous roads in this area. I have made my own trip as accurate as possible in detail. For a more complete mapping of roads use the Highway Department's Washington County map.
St. Peters Church
right on Johnson School Road
turn left at golf course
Minter Bridge Road
Burkhalter Road
Lewis Pioneer Cemetery 1847
BEAVERTON 8
Old schoolhouse
Rood Bridge Rd.
208
Riedwig Road
Simpson Road
turn right on road toward Scholls
OAK KNOLL WINERY
River Road
Old hop-curing house
PORTLAND 9
210
Vandermost Road
PONZI VINEYARDS


Roads to churches and vineyards of the Tualatin Plain

Certainly one of the most eye-catching of the Oregon churches I saw during my travels was The Old Scotch Church. I tried to approximate the charm of its setting of tall trees and green-lawned cemetery in this drawing.

At Roy I found another striking church with a silver tower shining in the sun.

The Old Scotch Church

I tasted one of winemaker Bill Fuller's excellent rieslings at Tualatin Vineyards. To mark the occasion I sketched this view from the vineyard of young vines to the Tualatin plain in the distance.

These back roads took me to four wineries in all (they are usually open to visitors on weekends) and past views of many fine churches along the way.

At the Dutch community of Verboordt the handsome Catholic church was surrounded by colossal redwood trees.

Tualatin Vineyards

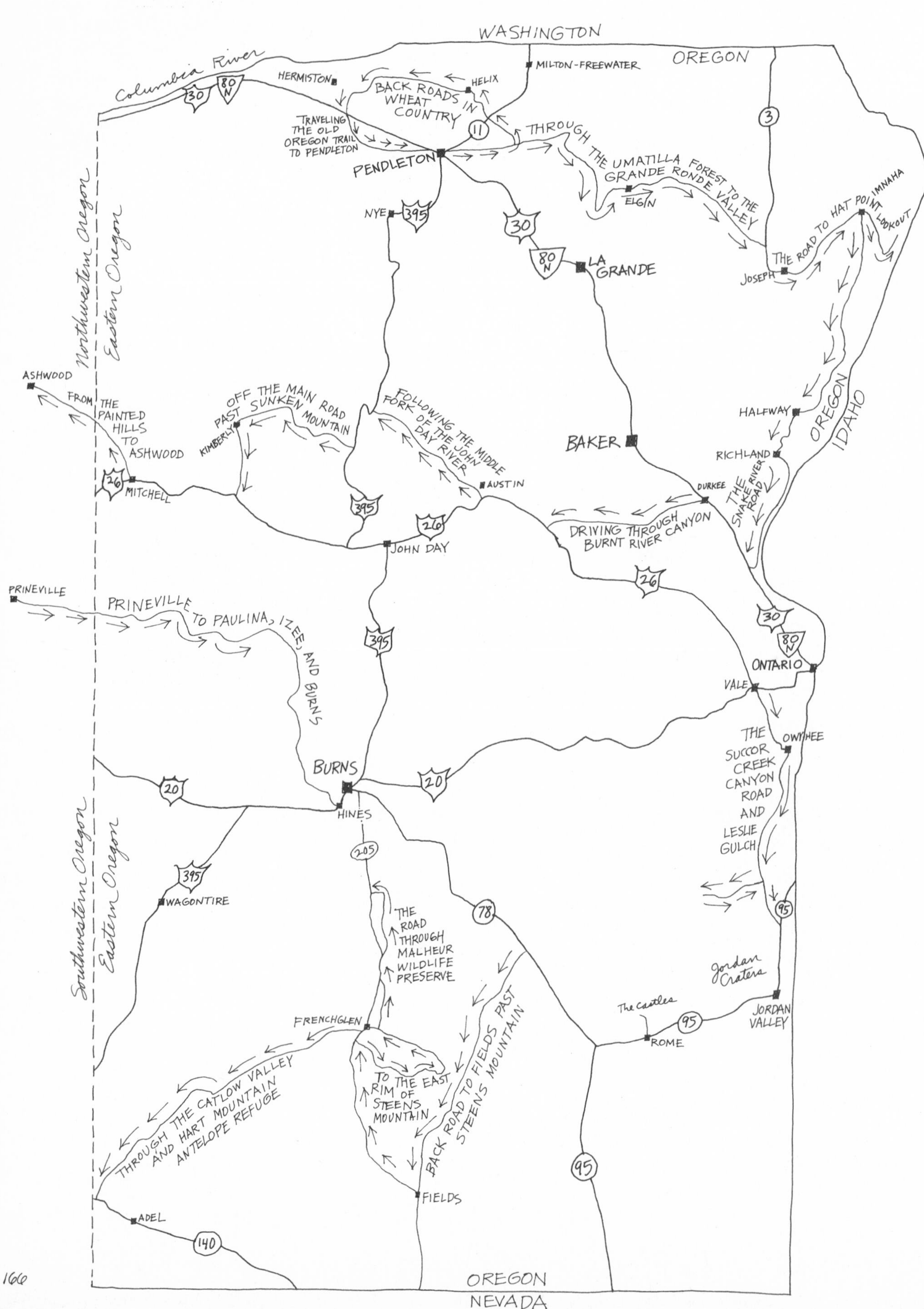
WASHINGTON
OREGON
Columbia River
HERMISTON
HELIX
MILTON-FREEWATER
BACK ROADS IN WHEAT COUNTRY
TRAVELING THE OLD OREGON TRAIL TO PENDLETON
PENDLETON
THROUGH THE UMATILLA FOREST TO THE GRANDE RONDE VALLEY
ELGIN
NYE
LA GRANDE
THE ROAD TO HAT POINT
IMNAHA
LOOKOUT
JOSEPH
Northwestern Oregon
Eastern Oregon
ASHWOOD
FROM THE PAINTED HILLS TO ASHWOOD
OFF THE MAIN ROAD PAST SUNKEN MOUNTAIN
KIMBERLY
FOLLOWING THE MIDDLE FORK OF THE JOHN DAY RIVER
BAKER
HALFWAY
RICHLAND
OREGON
IDAHO
THE SNAKE RIVER ROAD
MITCHELL
AUSTIN
DURKEE
DRIVING THROUGH BURNT RIVER CANYON
JOHN DAY
PRINEVILLE
PRINEVILLE TO PAULINA, IZEE, AND BURNS
ONTARIO
VALE
THE SUCCOR CREEK CANYON ROAD AND LESLIE GULCH
OWYHEE
BURNS
HINES
Southwestern Oregon
Eastern Oregon
WAGONTIRE
THE ROAD THROUGH MALHEUR WILDLIFE PRESERVE
Jordan Craters
The Castles
JORDAN VALLEY
ROME
FRENCHGLEN
THROUGH THE CATLOW VALLEY AND HART MOUNTAIN ANTELOPE REFUGE
TO THE EAST RIM OF STEENS MOUNTAIN
BACK ROAD TO FIELDS PAST STEENS MOUNTAIN
FIELDS
ADEL
OREGON
NEVADA

# Eastern Oregon

The immensity of this region's mountains, canyons, rivers, plains and gorges, stretching out under a huge expanse of sky challenged my comprehension. Back roads here were longer, dustier, and often bumpier than those in western Oregon, but they were nevertheless just as well worth traveling. And it was like entering the "real" west with its cattle, coyotes, antelope, dust devils, cowboys, and tumbling-down early settlers' cabins.

Sunflower, Snake River road

## Traveling the old Oregon Trail to Pendleton

Cara Neal said her barn had been painted with a Bull Durham slogan in 1911, but within a year Dr. Pierce came along with a better offer and the sign was painted over.

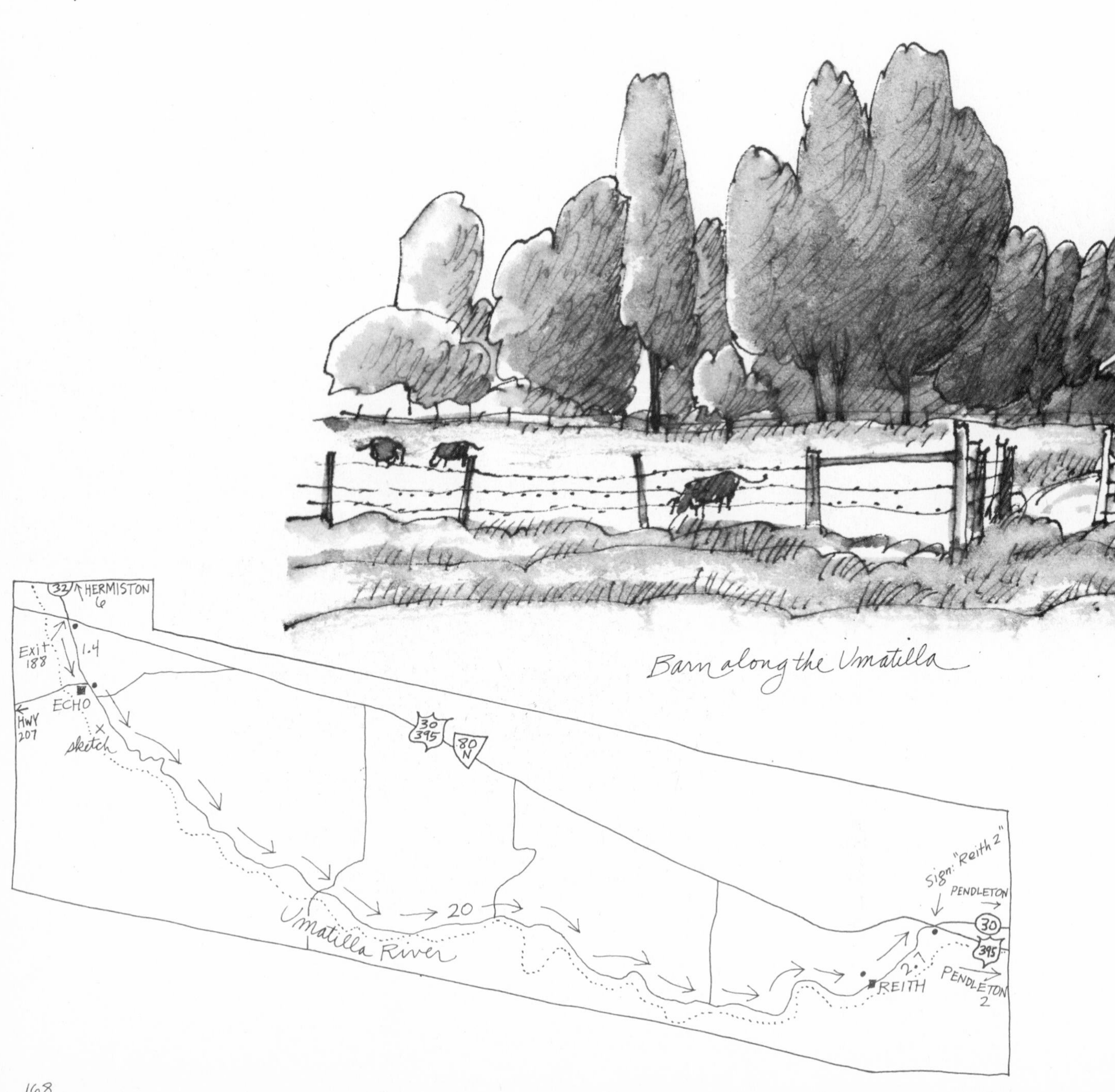
32
HERMISTON
6
Exit
188
1.4
ECHO
HWY
207
sketch
30
395
80
N
Umatilla River
20
Sign: "Reith 2"
PENDLETON
30
395
2.7
REITH
PENDLETON
2

Barn along the Umatilla

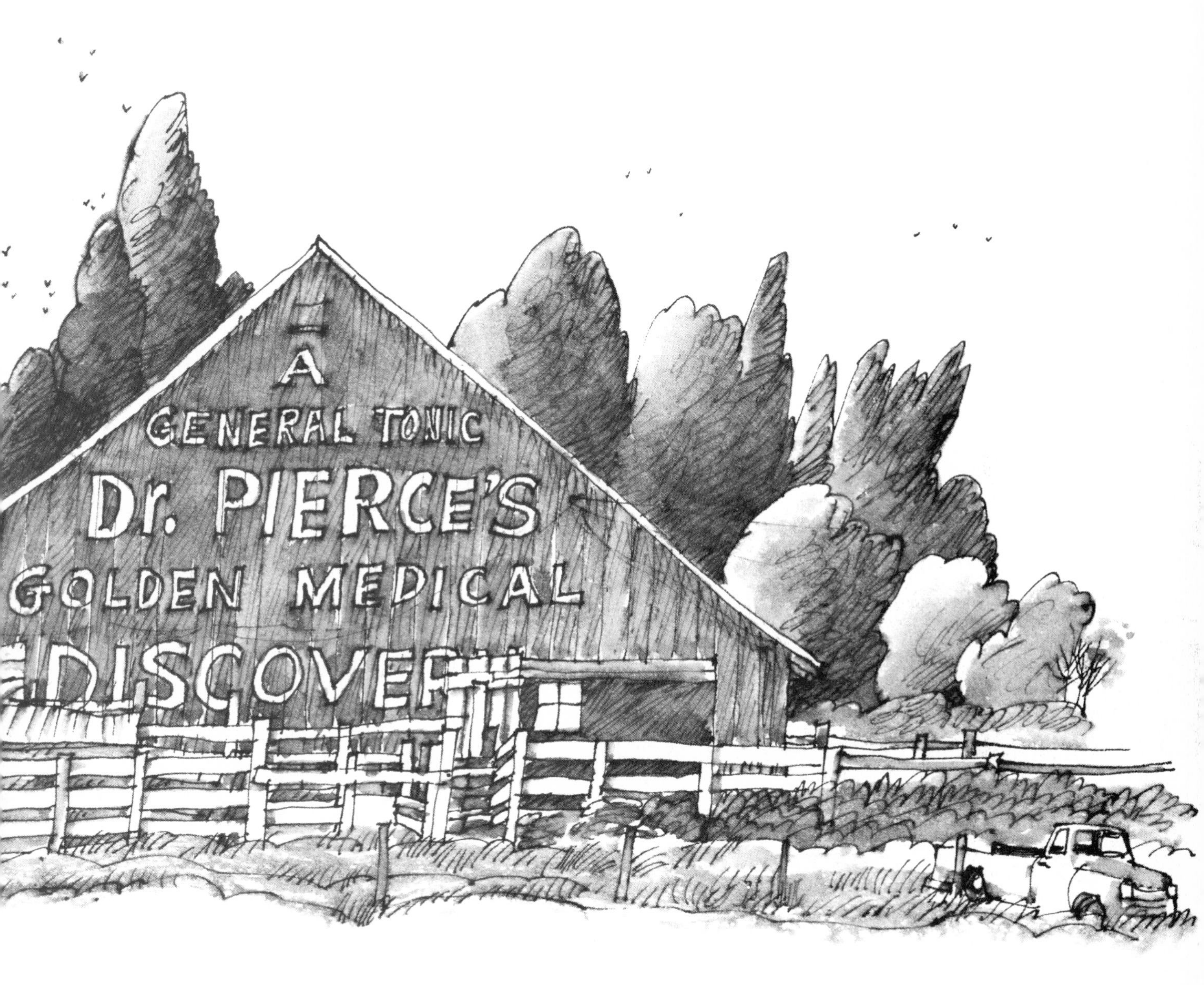
A
GENERAL TONIC
Dr. PIERCE'S
GOLDEN MEDICAL
DISCOVER

The road past Echo was once the main highway, but now only back road travelers can be apprised of the doctor's Golden Medical Discovery. The Umatilla runs past this road and so do long, long freight trains.

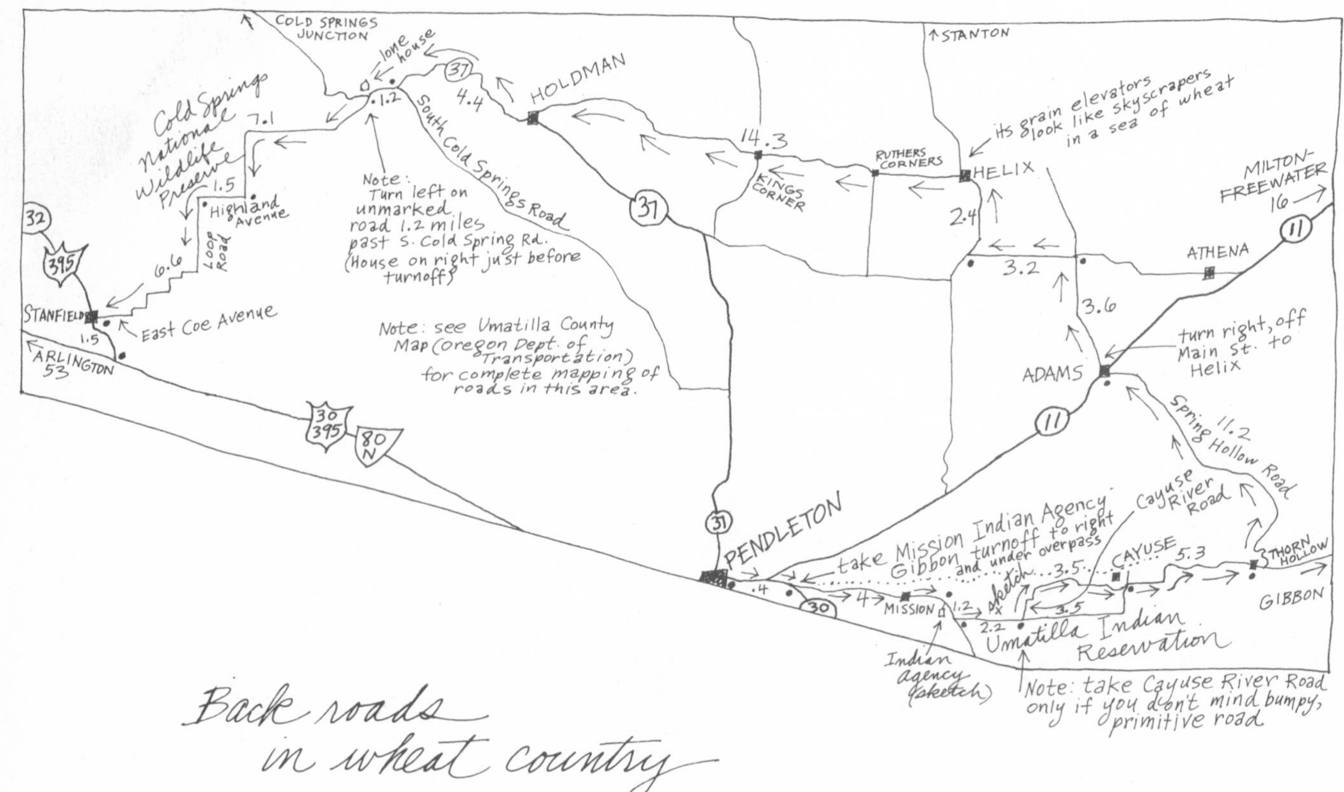

COLD SPRINGS JUNCTION
lone house
37
HOLDMAN
4.4
1.2
South Cold Springs Road
Cold Springs National Wildlife Preserve
7.1
1.5
Highland Avenue
Note: Turn left on unmarked road 1.2 miles past S. Cold Spring Rd. (House on right just before turnoff)
14.3
KINGS CORNER
RUTHERS CORNERS
STANTON
its grain elevators look like skyscrapers in a sea of wheat
HELIX
2.4
MILTON-FREEWATER 16
3.2
3.6
ATHENA
11
32
395
6.6
Loop Road
STANFIELD
East Coe Avenue
1.5
ARLINGTON 53
Note: see Umatilla County Map (Oregon Dept. of Transportation) for complete mapping of roads in this area.
turn right, off Main St. to Helix
ADAMS
30 395
80 N
11.2
Spring Hollow Road
Cayuse River Road
PENDLETON
take Mission Indian Agency-Gibbon turnoff to right and under overpass
.4
30
4
MISSION
1.2
2.2
sketch
3.5
3.5
CAYUSE
5.3
THORN HOLLOW
GIBBON
Umatilla Indian Reservation
Indian agency (sketch)
Note: take Cayuse River Road only if you don't mind bumpy, primitive road


## Back roads in wheat country

On these roads long views of wheat fields and the patterns that plowing them makes delighted my eyes.

A totem pole adorns the entrance to the Bureau of Interior Umatilla Indian Reservation. The Indian worker I asked about its origin said that it had been constructed in the early 1930s by CCC camp laborers at nearby Squaw Creek. The talents of many went into its creation. It has been repainted several times, noses have been replaced, and the base repaired, so that the CCC totem still stands tall at reservation headquarters.

Totem at the Umatilla Indian Agency

Wheat fields around Pendleton

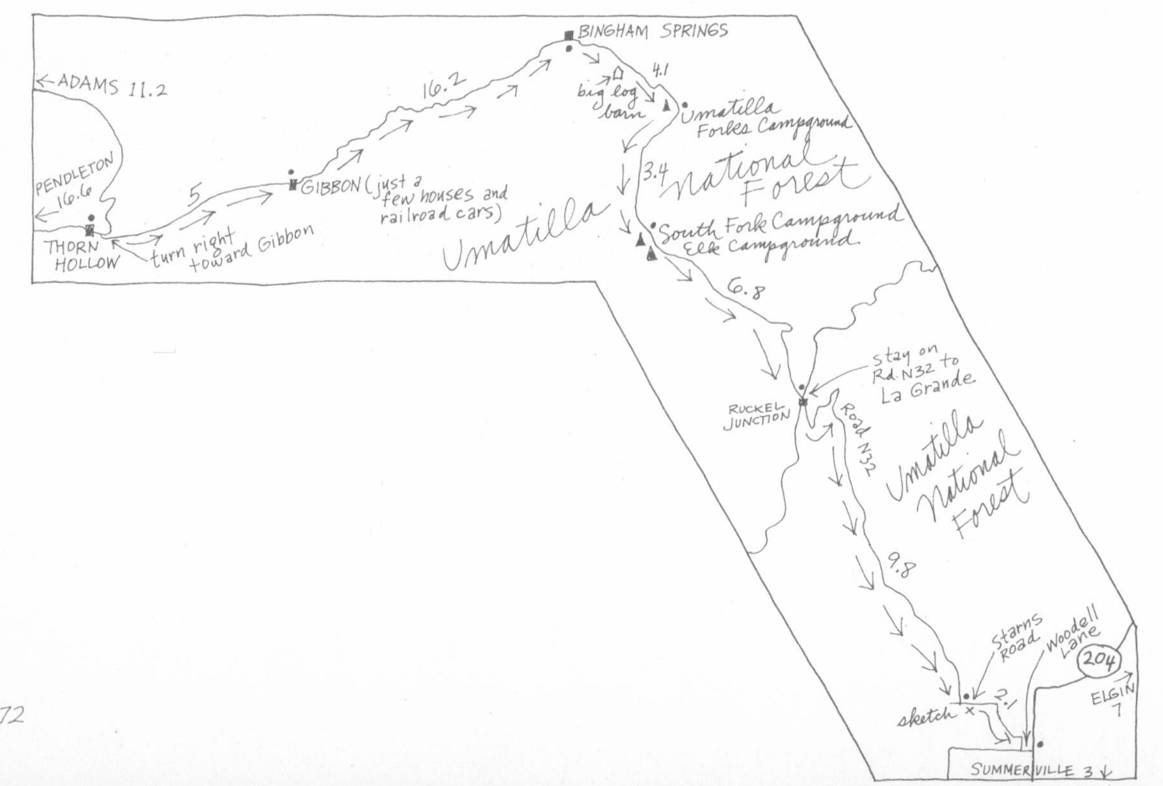

BINGHAM SPRINGS
←ADAMS 11.2
16.2
4.1
big log barn
Umatilla Forks Campground
PENDLETON 16.6
5
GIBBON (just a few houses and railroad cars)
3.4
National Forest
THORN HOLLOW
turn right toward Gibbon
Umatilla
South Fork Campground
Elk Campground
6.8
stay on Rd. N32 to La Grande
RUCKEL JUNCTION
Road N32
Umatilla National Forest
9.8
Starns Road
Woodell Lane
204
sketch
2.1
ELGIN 7
SUMMERVILLE 3

Through the Umatilla Forest to the Grande Ronde Valley

By the time I reached Gibbon, forest trees were beginning to appear. I passed Bingham Springs, where there once had been a sulphur springs spa, and the Bar M Ranch with its great log barn.

I continued on the mountain road through the forest to the spacious and fertile Grande Ronde Valley.

The Grande Ronde Valley

The road to
Hat Point Lookout

Stopping at the Ranger Station at Joseph to check on road conditions, I was handed a guide describing the trip to Hat Point. There was a popular store at Imnaha, where one could enjoy a cold drink before ascending to or descending from Hat Point. The road to the top was long and bumpy. The scenery, however, made it all worthwhile.

I climbed the 100 steps to the tiny cabin of Hat Point lookout tower where 7,072 feet above the earth's surface at sea level, I had a view of the Snake River in Hell's Canyon 1,250 feet below.

The view from Hat Point

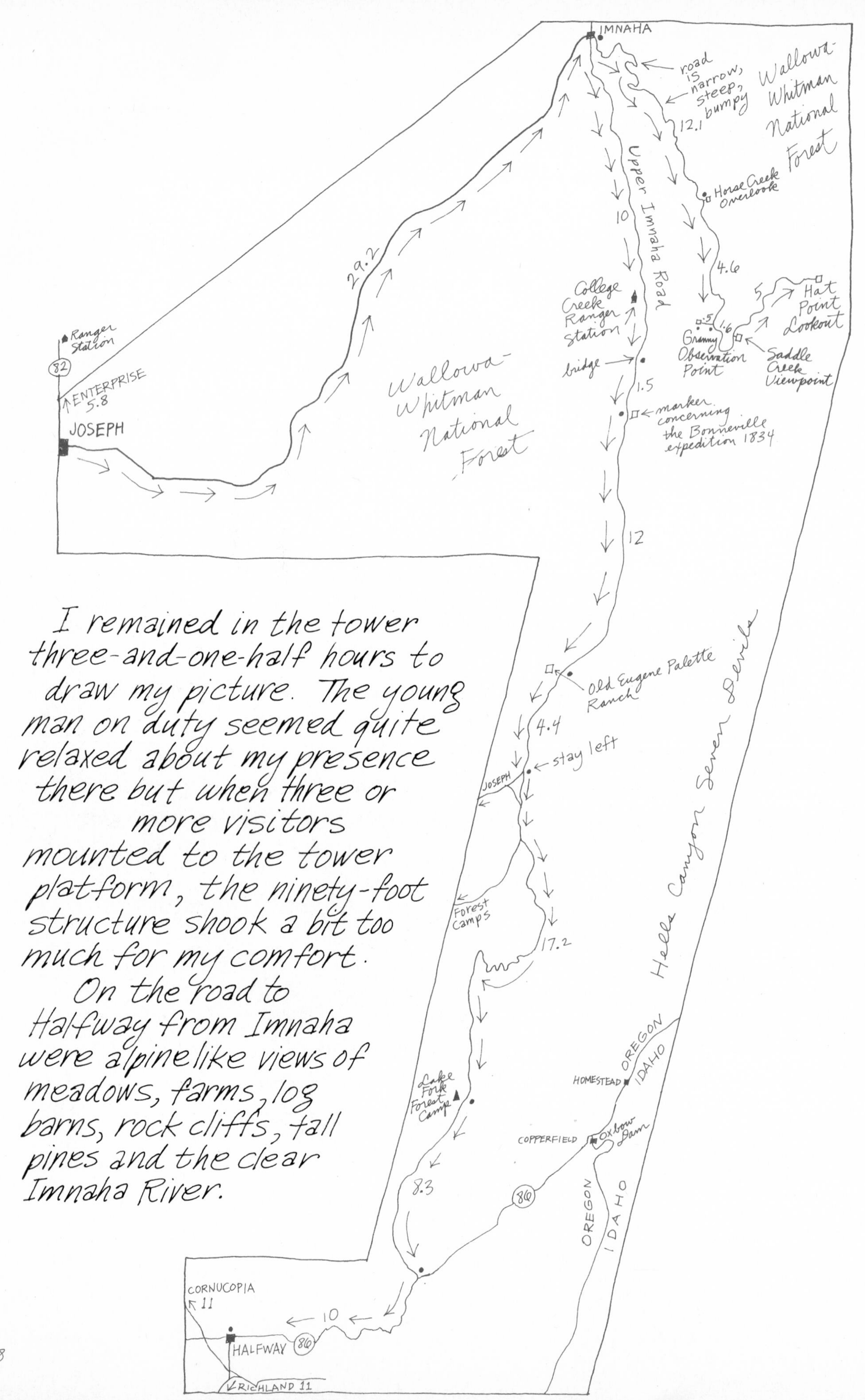
IMNAHA
road is narrow, steep, bumpy
12.1
Wallowa-Whitman National Forest
Upper Imnaha Road
10
Horse Creek Overlook
4.6
5
Hat Point Lookout
College Creek Ranger Station
bridge
.5
1.6
Granny Observation Point
Saddle Creek Viewpoint
1.5
marker concerning the Bonneville expedition 1834
29.2
Ranger Station
82
ENTERPRISE 5.8
JOSEPH
Wallowa-Whitman National Forest
12
Old Eugene Palette Ranch
4.4
stay left
JOSEPH
Forest camps
17.2
Hells Canyon Seven Devils
OREGON
IDAHO
HOMESTEAD
Lake Fork Forest Camp
COPPERFIELD
Oxbow Dam
86
8.3
OREGON
IDAHO
CORNUCOPIA 11
10
HALFWAY
86
RICHLAND 11

I remained in the tower three-and-one-half hours to draw my picture. The young man on duty seemed quite relaxed about my presence there but when three or more visitors mounted to the tower platform, the ninety-foot structure shook a bit too much for my comfort.

On the road to Halfway from Imnaha were alpinelike views of meadows, farms, log barns, rock cliffs, tall pines and the clear Imnaha River.

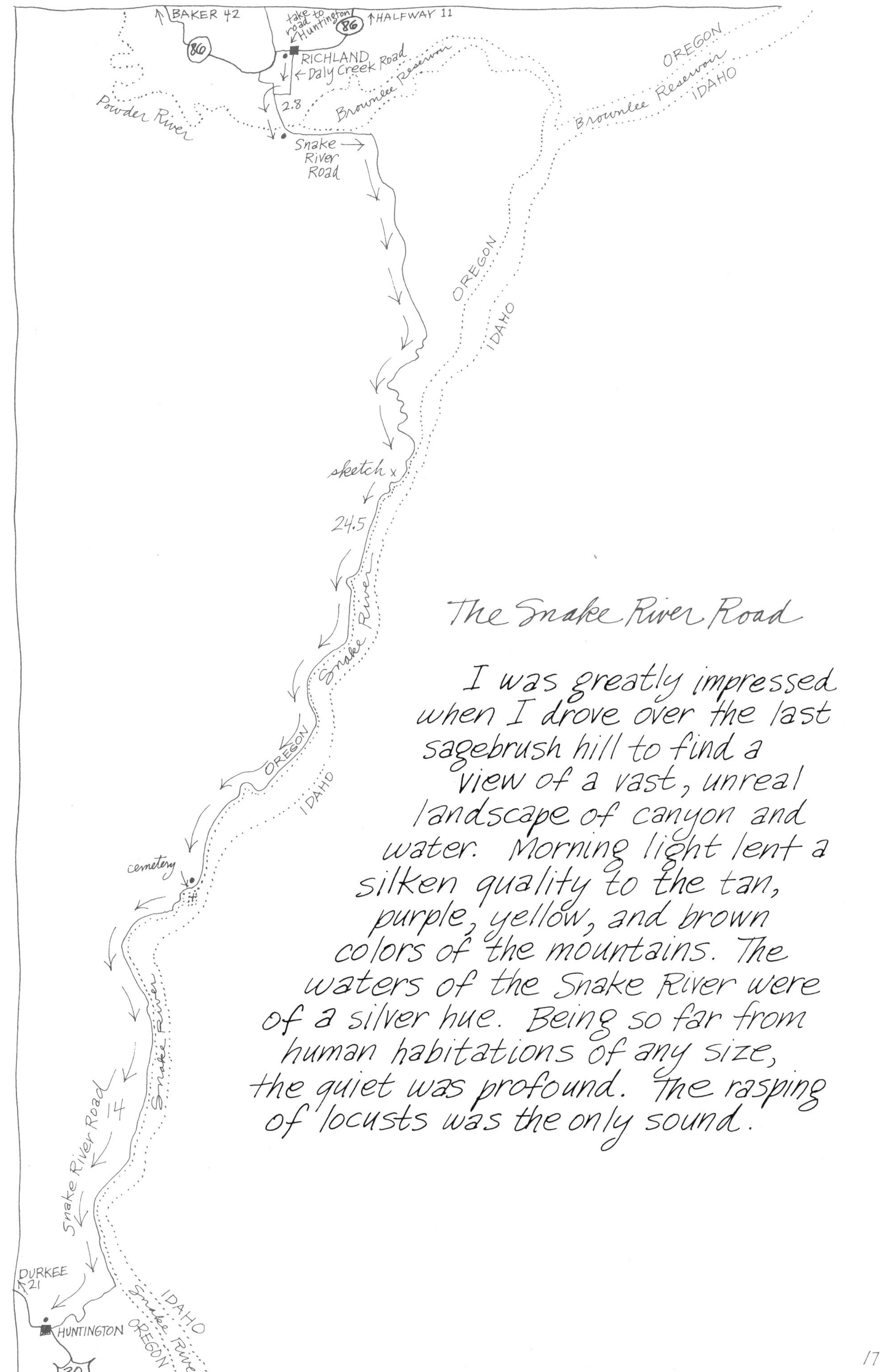
BAKER 42
take to road to Huntington
86
HALFWAY 11
RICHLAND
Daly Creek Road
Brownlee Reservoir
OREGON
IDAHO
Powder River
2.8
Snake River Road
sketch x
24.5
OREGON
IDAHO
Snake River
cemetery
14
Snake River Road
DURKEE 21
HUNTINGTON
30
ONTARIO 30

# The Snake River Road

I was greatly impressed when I drove over the last sagebrush hill to find a view of a vast, unreal landscape of canyon and water. Morning light lent a silken quality to the tan, purple, yellow, and brown colors of the mountains. The waters of the Snake River were of a silver hue. Being so far from human habitations of any size, the quiet was profound. The rasping of locusts was the only sound.

*The Snake River Road along the Oregon-Idaho border*

Giant blazing star

## Driving through Burnt River Canyon

I came upon many cattle and sage grouse along the road. The cattle would stare, then turn and trot ahead of me until I could gently overtake them and encourage them to one side. A cowboy rounding up a small herd told me "Ah'm jes' taken' 'em up the road."

I sketched a flower along here, the giant blazing star, which has five white starlike petals that open at night.

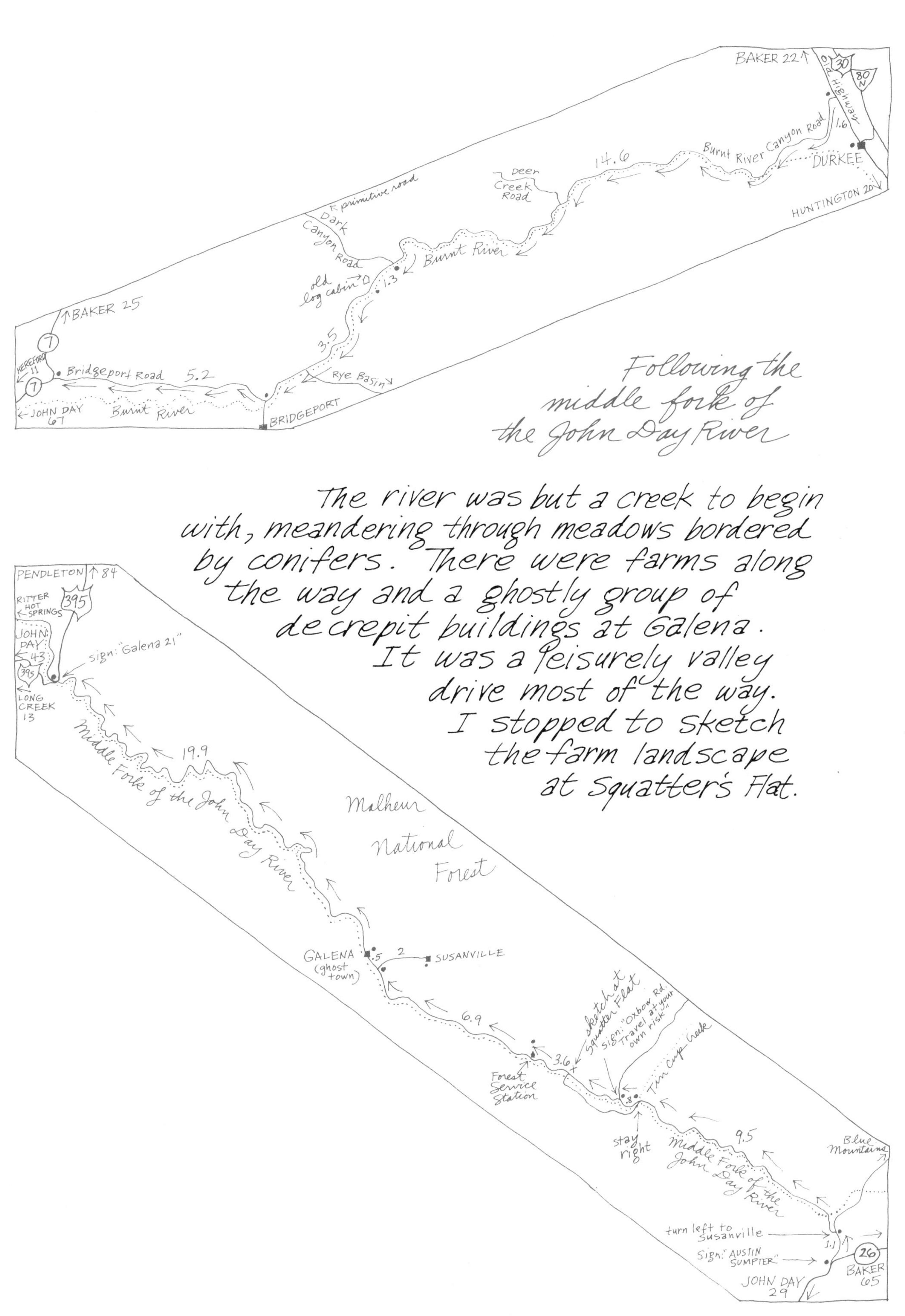
BAKER 22
Old Highway
30
80 N
1.6
DURKEE
HUNTINGTON 20
Burnt River Canyon Road
14.6
Deer Creek Road
Burnt River
primitive road
Dark Canyon Road
old log cabin
1.3
BAKER 25
7
HEREFORD 11
7
Bridgeport Road
5.2
3.5
Rye Basin
BRIDGEPORT
JOHN DAY 67
Burnt River
PENDLETON 84
395
RITTER HOT SPRINGS
JOHN DAY 43
395
LONG CREEK 13
sign: "Galena 21"
19.9
Middle Fork of the John Day River
Malheur National Forest
GALENA (ghost town)
.5
2
SUSANVILLE
6.9
Forest Service Station
3.6
sketch at Squatter Flat
sign: "Oxbow Rd. Travel at your own risk."
Tin Cup Creek
.8
stay right
9.5
Middle Fork of the John Day River
Blue Mountains
turn left to Susanville
1.1
Sign: "AUSTIN SUMPTER"
26
BAKER 65
JOHN DAY 29

# *Following the middle fork of the John Day River*

The river was but a creek to begin with, meandering through meadows bordered by conifers. There were farms along the way and a ghostly group of decrepit buildings at Galena. It was a leisurely valley drive most of the way. I stopped to sketch the farm landscape at Squatter's Flat.

Farm at Squatter's Flat along the middle fork of the John Day River

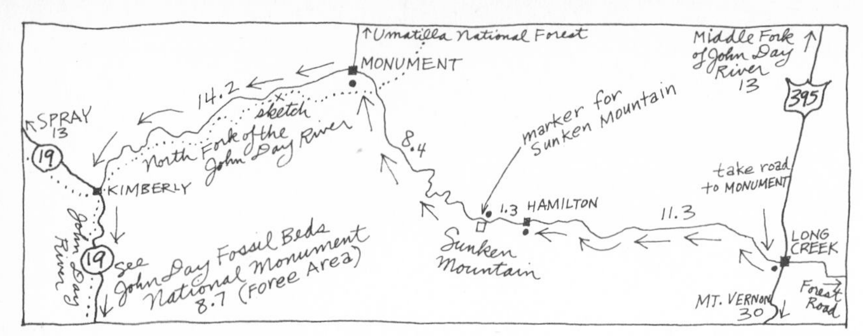
Umatilla National Forest
MONUMENT
Middle Fork of John Day River 13
395
14.2
sketch
SPRAY 13
19
North Fork of the John Day River
8.4
marker for Sunken Mountain
KIMBERLY
take road to MONUMENT
1.3
HAMILTON
11.3
John Day River
19
See John Day Fossil Beds National Monument 8.7 (Foree Area)
Sunken Mountain
LONG CREEK
MT. VERNON 30
Forest Road

## *Off the main road past Sunken Mountain*

In Oregon some back roads are much like highways. This fast back road passed a view of Sunken Mountain, which, did indeed seem to slip in the middle. The slow-paced village of Monument is surrounded by impressive rock formations. Just beyond the town I sketched the north fork of the John Day River as it flowed through the mountains.

*North fork of the John Day River, near Monument*

## From the Painted Hills to Ashwood

I drew the ochres, yellows and reds of Painted Hills in the early morning. It was a challenge to represent so much color in black and white!

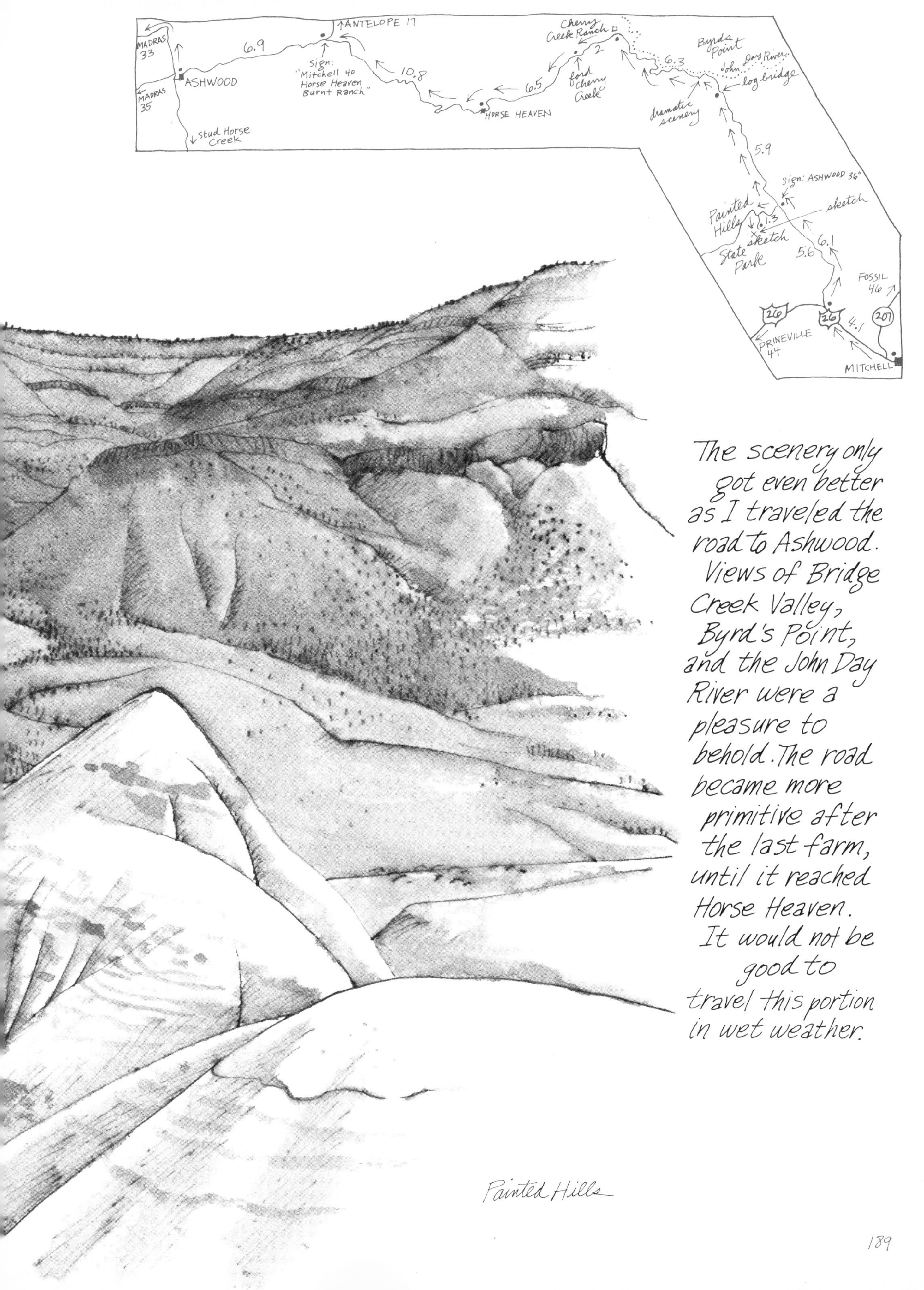

MADRAS 33
ANTELOPE 17
6.9
Sign: "Mitchell 40 Horse Heaven Burnt Ranch"
10.8
Cherry Creek Ranch
2
ford Cherry Creek
6.5
HORSE HEAVEN
ASHWOOD
MADRAS 35
Stud Horse Creek
Byrds Point
John Day River
6.3
log bridge
dramatic scenery
5.9
Sign: ASHWOOD 36"
sketch
Painted Hills
1.3
sketch
State Park
5.6
6.1
FOSSIL 46
26
26
4.1
207
PRINEVILLE 44
MITCHELL


The scenery only got even better as I traveled the road to Ashwood. Views of Bridge Creek Valley, Byrd's Point, and the John Day River were a pleasure to behold. The road became more primitive after the last farm, until it reached Horse Heaven. It would not be good to travel this portion in wet weather.

Painted Hills

## Prineville to Paulina, Izee and Burns

There was the Crooked River, farmland, and the mountains of Ochoco National Forest to see on this trip.

At Glenn Place near Paulina I sat in the shade of tall Lombardy poplars to sketch.

A great horned owl peered out by the window of the historic old log house. It didn't fly off but remained to keep a blinking eye on me.

Paulina had a frontier town look with its little church and assortment of houses clustered near the General Store.

Glenn Place

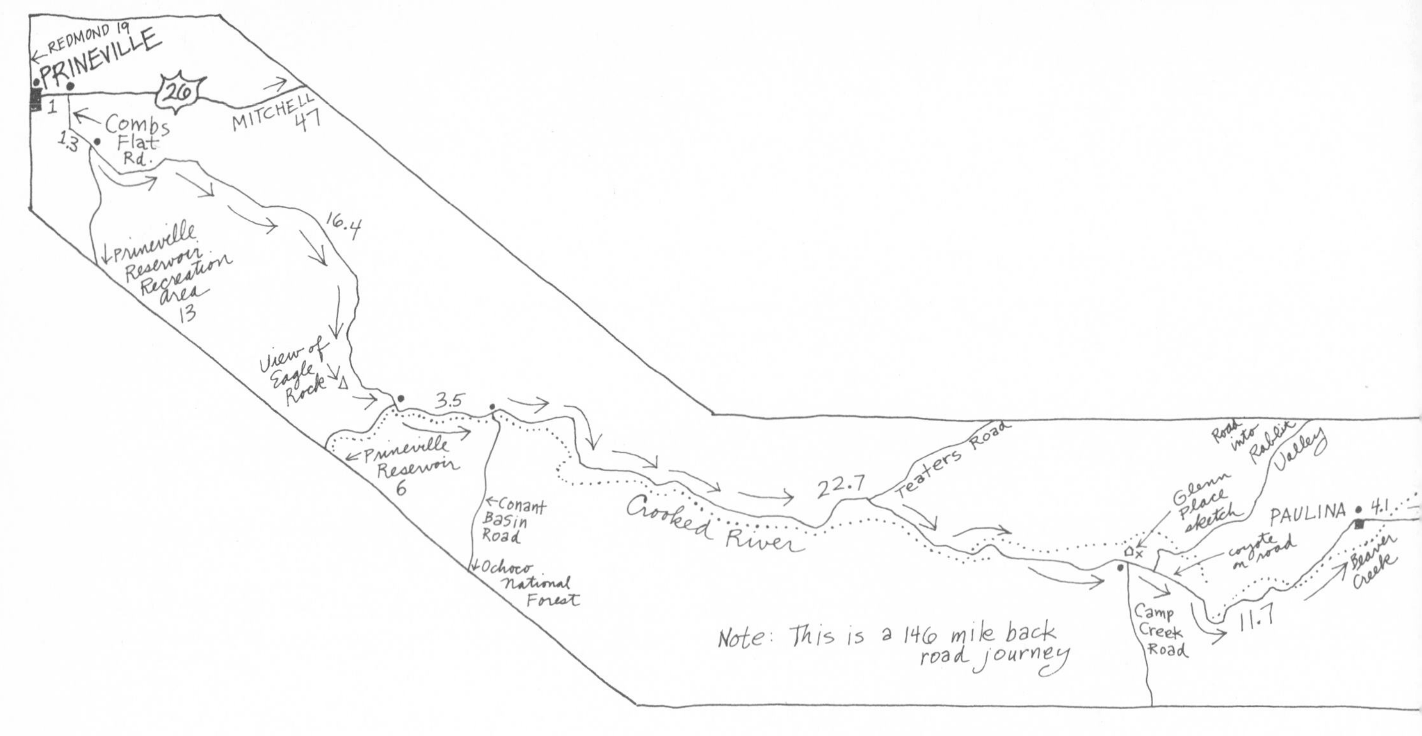
REDMOND 19
PRINEVILLE
26
MITCHELL 47
1
1.3
Combs Flat Rd.
16.4
Prineville Reservoir Recreation Area 13
View of Eagle Rock
3.5
Prineville Reservoir 6
Conant Basin Road
Ochoco National Forest
Crooked River
22.7
Teaters Road
Road into Rabbit Valley
Glenn Place sketch
PAULINA
4.1
coyote on road
Beaver Creek
Camp Creek Road
11.7
Note: This is a 146 mile back road journey

## The Succor Creek Canyon Road and Leslie Gulch

The scenery was rugged with purplish brown crags that surrounded us campers in Succor Creek Canyon. It was late in the day. I cooked some dinner at the campground and watched the moon go down behind the high canyon walls. The only sound was cooing of doves from their perches among the high rocks.

Early next morning on the way to Leslie Gulch a herd of deer, including four large bucks, bounded gracefully across the road.

Leslie Gulch was a magnificent natural cathedral offering a treasury of highly colored and lofty rock creations for me to enjoy.

There were also the Jordan Craters close to the town of Jordan Valley and, near Rome, "the castles" to see.

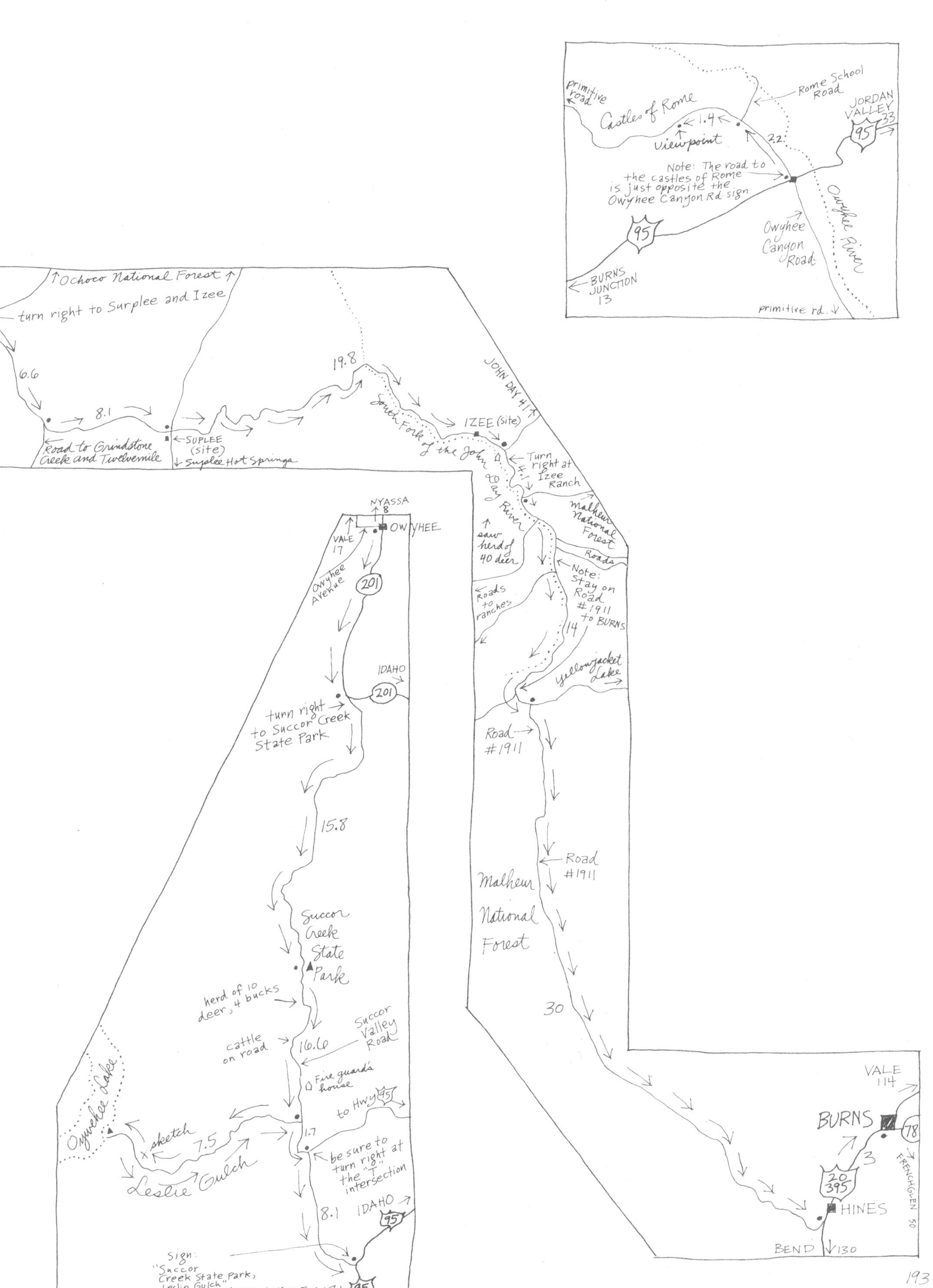
primitive road
Castles of Rome
1.4
Viewpoint
Rome School Road
JORDAN VALLEY 33
95
2.2
Note: The road to the castles of Rome is just opposite the Owyhee Canyon Rd. sign
Owyhee River
Owyhee Canyon Road
95
BURNS JUNCTION 13
primitive rd.
Ochoco National Forest
turn right to Surplee and Izee
6.6
8.1
Road to Grindstone Creek and Twelvemile
SUPLEE (site)
Suplee Hot Springs
19.8
JOHN DAY 41
South Fork of the John Day River
IZEE (site)
Turn right at Izee Ranch
Malheur National Forest
Roads
saw herd of 40 deer
Roads to ranches
Note: Stay on Road #1911 to BURNS
14
Yellowjacket Lake
Road #1911
Road #1911
Malheur National Forest
30
VALE 114
BURNS
78
3
20
395
FRENCHGLEN 50
HINES
BEND 130
NYASSA 8
VALE 17
OWYHEE
Owyhee Avenue
201
IDAHO
201
turn right to Succor Creek State Park
15.8
Succor Creek State Park
herd of 10 deer, 4 bucks
cattle on road
16.6
Succor Valley Road
Fire guard's house
to Hwy 95
Owyhee Lake
sketch
7.5
Leslie Gulch
1.7
be sure to turn right at the "T" intersection
8.1
IDAHO
95
Sign: "Succor Creek State Park, Leslie Gulch"
JORDAN VALLEY 18
95

Leslie Gulch

Back road to Fields
past Steen's Mountain

The great mass of Steen's Mountain rose to incredible heights from the valley floor along this road. There were occasional farms, and the large Alvord Ranch. I found it comforting to know that I wasn't entirely alone on this sixty-five-mile stretch of dirt road!

Farther on there was a big, big view of the Alvord Desert and the mighty 9,000-foot Steen's Mountain towering above.

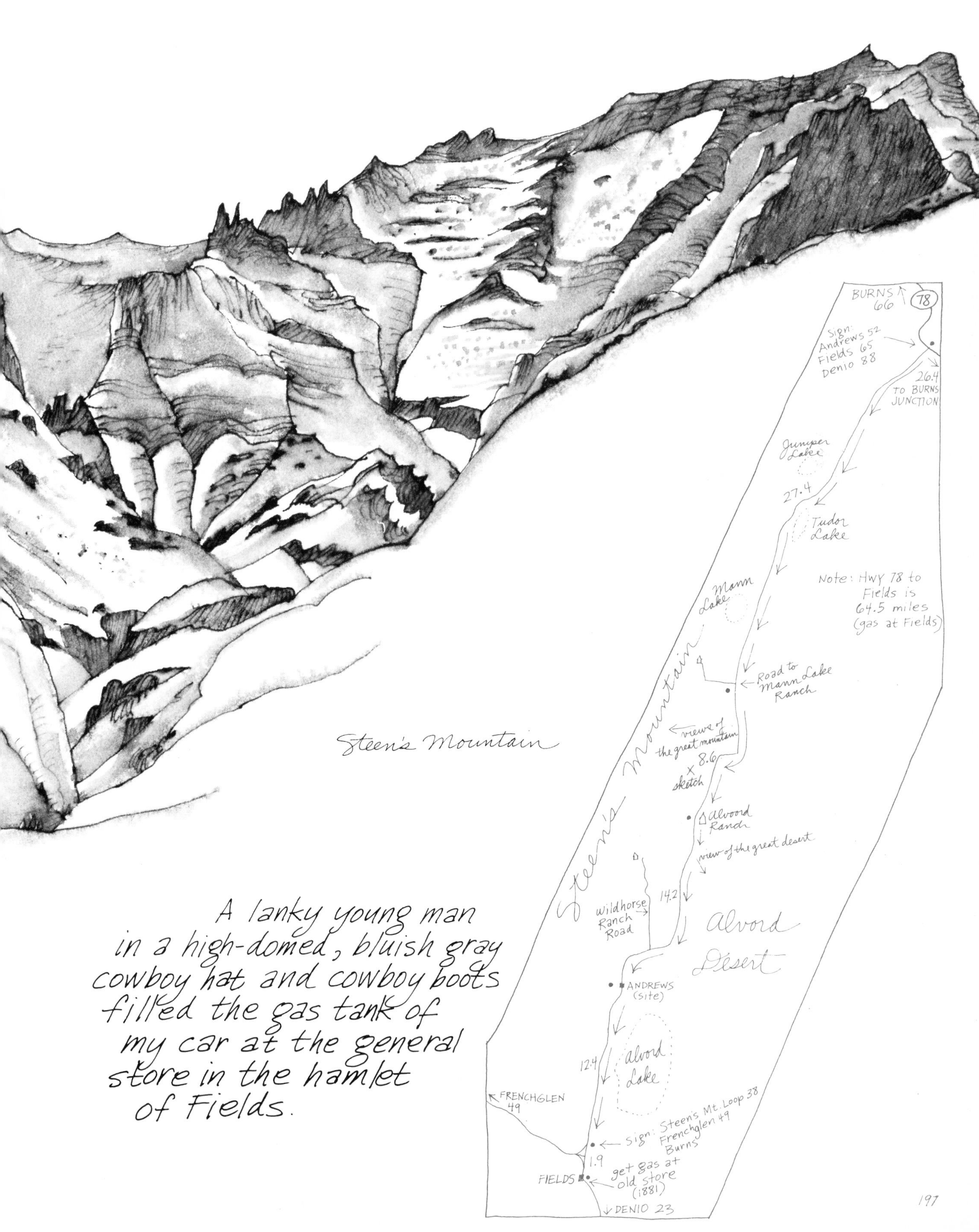
Steen's Mountain
BURNS 66
78
Sign: Andrews 52 Fields 65 Denio 88
26.4 TO BURNS JUNCTION
Juniper Lake
27.4
Tudor Lake
Note: Hwy 78 to Fields is 64.5 miles (gas at Fields)
Mann Lake
Road to Mann Lake Ranch
Steen's Mountain
views of the great mountain
8.6
sketch
Alvord Ranch
view of the great desert
14.2
Wildhorse Ranch Road
Alvord Desert
ANDREWS (site)
12.4
Alvord Lake
FRENCHGLEN 49
Sign: Steen's Mt. Loop 38 Frenchglen 49 Burns
1.9
FIELDS
get gas at old store (1881)
DENIO 23

A lanky young man in a high-domed, bluish gray cowboy hat and cowboy boots filled the gas tank of my car at the general store in the hamlet of Fields.

# To the east rim of Steen's Mountain

At the base of the Steen's Mountain Loop was the tiny community of Frenchglen and its comfortable hotel. Still in operation, it was built in 1916 by the famous local cattle baron of that time, Pete French.

The drive up Steen's Mountain was deceptive in that it was such a gradual slope I didn't realize I was achieving great altitude. Passing from sagebrush country to juniper, to groves of aspen and to alpine wildflower strewn meadow told me I was certainly gaining altitude. Higher up there were spectacular views of glaciated valleys and from the east rim the large vista of the Alvord Desert over a mile below and all the land beyond.

BURNS 60
FRENCHGLEN
3.4
6.9
205
Hart Mountain
Antelope Refuge 35
Page Glen Campground
15.4
2.8 miles to Kiger Gorge view
Start Steen's Mountain Road here (one way)
Jackman Park Campground
4.2
East Rim View
5
16.9
herd of 15 wild horses
South Rim Road 13.8
Roaring Springs Ranch
South Rim
Blitzen Crossing
9,600'
35.4
Steen's Mountain
HWY 78 64.5
1.4
FIELDS
DENIO 23

FRENCHGLEN
HOTEL

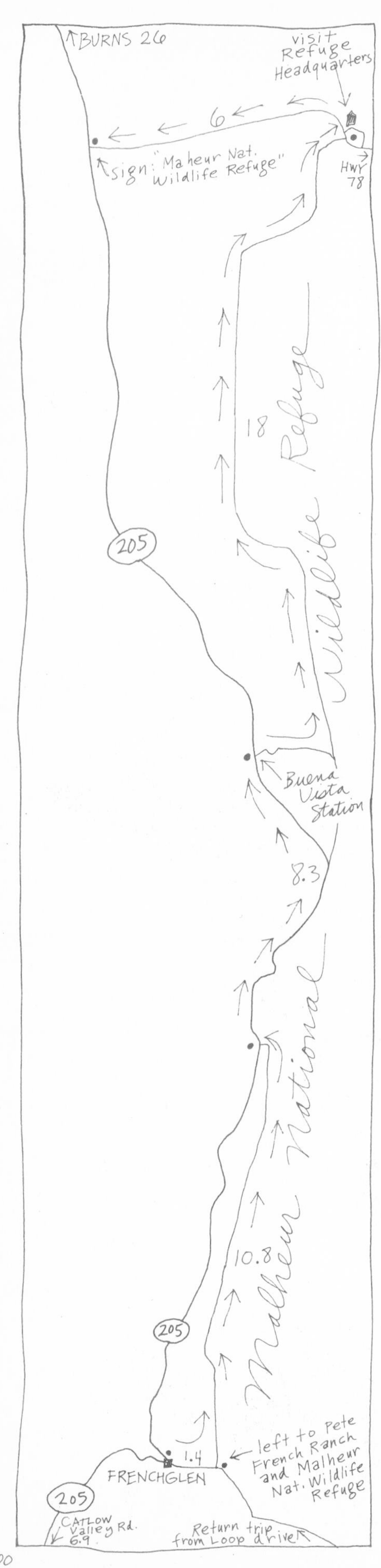
BURNS 26
visit Refuge Headquarters
6
sign: "Malheur Nat. Wildlife Refuge"
HWY 78
18
Malheur National Wildlife Refuge
205
Buena Vista Station
8.3
10.8
205
1.4
left to Pete French Ranch and Malheur Nat. Wildlife Refuge
FRENCHGLEN
205
CATLOW Valley Rd. 6.9
Return trip from Loop drive

## The road through Malheur Wildlife Refuge

Though it was not March or April, when the largest concentrations of birds are present, I was able to see many varieties. These included Great Blue Herons, White Pelicans, Trumpeter Swans, Canada Geese, Long-billed Curlews, Great Egrets, Snowy Egrets, and many kinds of ducks and hawks.

President Theodore Roosevelt established this preserve in 1908. Ponds and crops are managed for the benefit of wildlife.

It was good to see a place dedicated to man's concern for nature. What would our earth be like without birds of all variety?

Trumpeter Swan

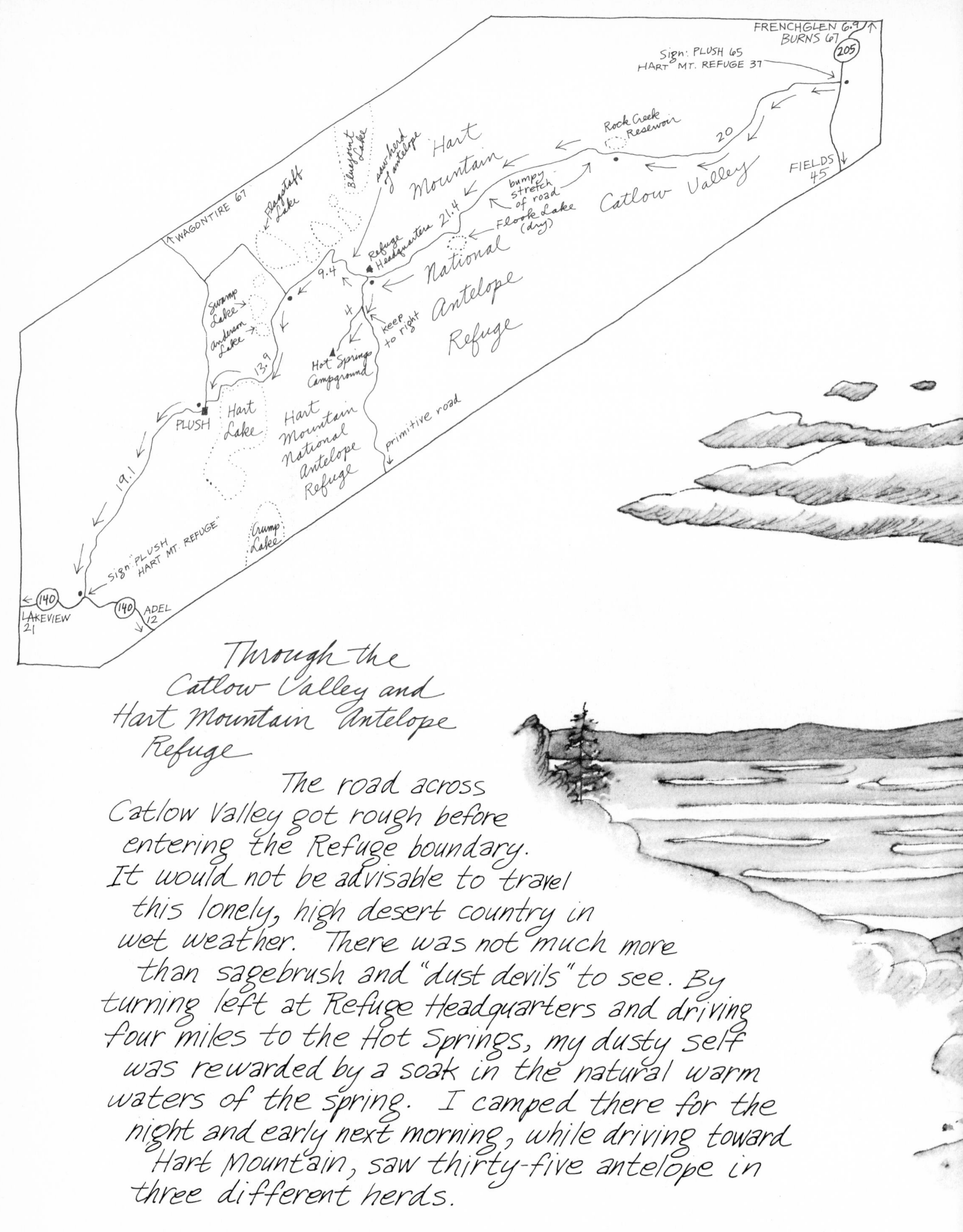

FRENCHGLEN 6.9
BURNS 67
205
Sign: PLUSH 65
HART MT. REFUGE 37
Rock Creek Reservoir
20
FIELDS 45
Catlow Valley
bumpy stretch of road
Flook Lake (dry)
Hart Mountain
saw herd of antelope
Bluejoint Lake
Flagstaff Lake
WAGONTIRE 67
Refuge Headquarters 21.4
9.4
National Antelope Refuge
Swamp Lake
Anderson Lake
4
Keep to right
Hot Springs Campground
13.9
PLUSH
Hart Lake
Hart Mountain National Antelope Refuge
primitive road
19.1
Crump Lake
Sign: PLUSH
HART MT. REFUGE"
140
LAKEVIEW 21
ADEL 12


# Through the Catlow Valley and Hart Mountain Antelope Refuge

The road across Catlow Valley got rough before entering the Refuge boundary. It would not be advisable to travel this lonely, high desert country in wet weather. There was not much more than sagebrush and "dust devils" to see. By turning left at Refuge Headquarters and driving four miles to the Hot Springs, my dusty self was rewarded by a soak in the natural warm waters of the spring. I camped there for the night and early next morning, while driving toward Hart Mountain, saw thirty-five antelope in three different herds.

Frightened by my vehicle they would run, then abruptly change direction, as if to confuse a hunter's aim. It was a thrill to see such beautiful animals in the wild.

View from Hart Mountain

Otis, my back
road advisor

## Thoughts while traveling

It adds much to the remembrance of a place to talk to local people. They would often introduce themselves to me while I was sketching, an opportunity to talk that I always welcomed.

I would also stop in the General Store to shop and perhaps quench my thirst by drinking something on the spot, returning the empty bottle to the counter. Sometimes just being in a place for awhile generates conversation. Checking road directions or getting advice on what to see locally is another usually successful way to begin a conversation with a stranger.

I believe that if one loves the earth and respects mankind one does not defile the land by throwing litter from an automobile.

I stayed in many motels in my travels through Oregon and those I appreciated most were neat, clean smelling and located away from highway noise. The owner's friendliness, flowers in the room (even just one or two) and a picture on the wall of good quality would make my home away from home all I could ask for.

Coming off a slow back road trip onto a busy highway, it is sometimes shocking to realize how fast and recklessly we have suddenly begun to travel.

I've become aware that the faster I drive the more I become an asphalt watcher. Driving is especially interesting and fun at slow speeds, for then I can enjoy the scenery. If there are many curves in the road I simply slow down even more. And on back roads I've noticed that many other drivers also seem to relax and enjoy the drive and the sights.

I'm remembering the route to Olallie Lake, a bumpy and twisted single lane road. The scenery was so close I could almost touch it. Ten miles per hour was maximum speed and though it was a narrow road, I knew that any traffic coming toward me was also limited by that speed so there was little likelihood of an accident.

I hope that road never changes. As soon as pavement and a double lane are put in, the road will be straightened, speed increased, and we will once again become asphalt watchers.

On dirt and gravel back roads I slowed down when meeting another vehicle to minimize the dust. I hoped that other drivers would do the same. Most often they did and we would both wave a greeting as we passed.

I wish more of Oregon's scenic back roads were in the one-way direction. Then they would not have to be wide, and more contact with nature would be felt. I'm thinking of the Grayback Ridge Motor Nature Trail near Crater Lake, a one-way road where I enjoyed a relaxing drive. I had more time to take in the sights than I would have otherwise. As Oregon's back roads are broadened and straightened for the needs of commerce, nature seems to retreat on all sides.

I found that many other drivers on back roads will wave as they go by. This is particularly true on less traveled roads. It is a wonderful way to indicate friendliness when an exchange of words isn't possible.

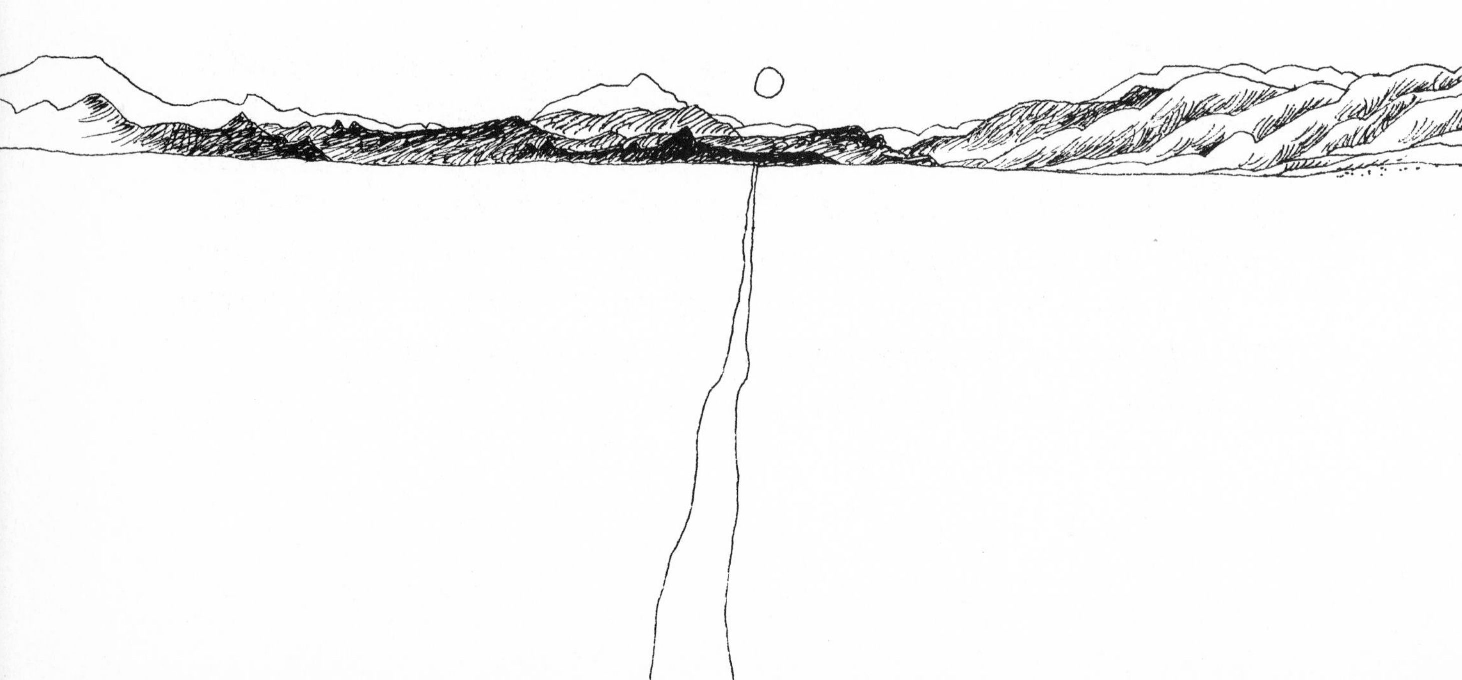

While I was sketching the Painted Hills, a young man stopped his car, snapped a picture with his camera, and drove away. It made me feel fortunate for my way of recording what I see. When he arrived, I had been drawing and observing for only a half-hour and my mind and body had already received much from the experience. There is a rapport with nature that occurs when I stop at a beautiful location long enough to draw. A feeling of peace enfolds me, and I seem to be truly interacting with the earth. (That is, at least until I drop ink on the paper, the temperature becomes intolerable, or ants crawl up my legs and bite.)

As functional and practical as they are, mobile homes are sometimes jarring to my sense of aesthetics. This is especially so when I see one prominently fixed in some lovely Oregon meadow or next to an elegant barn. I immediately feel like stopping to plant shrubs, trees, and flowers, to somewhat shroud its all too "box-car-looking" proportions.

Some owners of property along the back roads have posted large, forbidding "No Trespassing" signs. The reason for this is mostly an intense fear of grass or forest fires that could be started innocently enough by hikers or hunters who smoke, or campers who leave untended fires. We should all respect the demands of private property where they appear.

## Epilogue

Oregon was a truly varied, beautiful, and inspiring state to visit via the back roads.

I'm concerned about the preservation of our earth and have concluded that progress can only be defined in terms of how close we can come to living in harmony with nature. At a time when mankind has so many earth-destroying processes going on we often seem to be moving backward rather than ahead, Oregon has remained relatively unspoiled.

I believe that in order to advance and develop as a proud nation we need to restore the elemental beauty and purpose of nature, make healthy and pure our air and water, and preserve Oregon's and our heritage and history wherever and whenever possible. The needs of the planet earth should now supersede those of mankind.

Earl Thollander

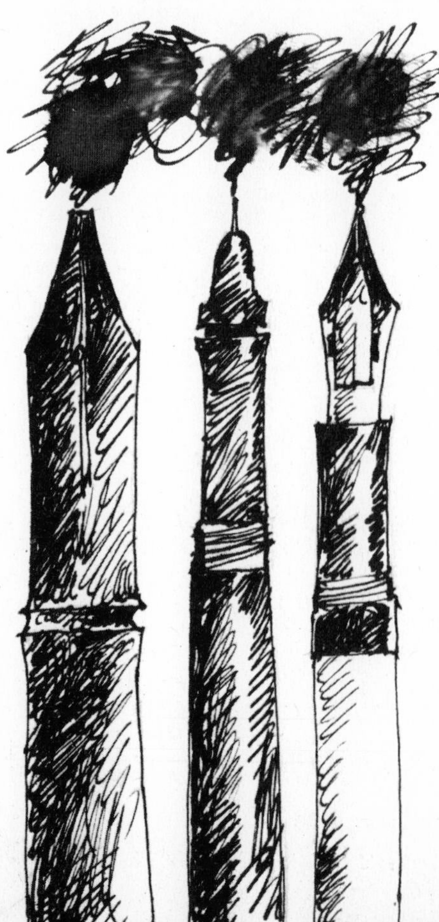

Thanks to artist John Simpkins and son Wes Thollander who were welcome company on my 6,000 mile back road journey through Oregon.